Praise for *Creative Juices*

Creative Juices is a beautiful gift. Like seasons in the garden, there are seasons in the writing life. Seasons for fully immersing oneself in the care and cultivation of writing. And then seasons for tending it a little at a time. *Creative Juices* is for both seasons. From her decades of practice as a writer, teacher and coach, Cynthia offers writers something rare: a manual both broad in scope, yet deep in writing soul. What Cynthia calls "snackable content" is truly her humble wisdom presented in an accessible way. Her words read as both meditation and call to action. I highly commend *Creative Juices* to the writing community.

—SHARI L. DRAGOVICH; food & culture writer, author of
The Texas Tavern: Four Generations of the Millionaire's Club

Creative Juices is brimming with writing wisdom and encouragement. Cynthia has somehow condensed a writers' conference and a personal coaching session into a single, readable book. If you write, buy this book.

—JOSH MOSEY, author of *3-Minute Prayers for Boys*
and co-founder of the Jot Conference

Creative Juices is an absolute must read for anyone who wants to write, but thinks they can't. It is packed with nourishment for the writer's soul and all the daily essentials for the writing life.

—SUSAN TEBOS, *Before You Were Mine: Discovering Your Adopted Child's Lifestory*

Cynthia Beach gifts writers with a resource filled with challenge, advice, encouragement and tools to help writers at all levels. *Creative Juices* is a treasure that will revamp and revitalize all areas of your writing life from soul care to characterization, from plot to process. Not to be missed!

—ANN BYLE, *Christian Publishing 101*

Cynthia Beach's *Creative Juices* is kicky and fun and does just what it says: it splashes the dry artistic soul with just the right juices. We're lucky to have this lively fruit from so many years of Ms. Beach's knowledge and experience.

—LESLIE LEYLAND FIELDS, *The Wonder Years: 40 Women Over 40 on
Aging, Faith, Beauty & Strength*

CREATIVE JUICES

A Splash of Story Craft, Process and Creative Soul Care

CYNTHIA BEACH

DEDICATION
To my fellow schopes

Cover design: David Frees
Cover art credit: iStock.com/Splash, Theeradech Sanin/Slices, anna1311
Interior design: Calli Mueller, Creatively Inclined
Editors: Amy Nemecek, Julie Schwab, McKenna Walter
Author photo credit: Rob Keys
Made and printed in the United States by
Color House Graphics, Grand Rapids, Michigan

Library of Congress Control Number: 2019904531
ISBN 978-0-692-03980-9

CONTENTS

Section IV: Craft Pizzazz

ACKNOWLEDGMENTS

Writing is a team sport, and I have many to thank. Mom who led me into reading by taking me again and again to libraries. Dad who taught me to reject the notion of "can't." Teachers and professors who wooed me to writing: Mary Kay Quinn, Dr. Judith Fabisch, David Egner, Dr. Mark Fackler, Wayne Ude and Bruce Holland Rogers. My writing companions: Noël Seif, Sharon Garlough Brown and the Guild—Ann Byle, Sharron Carrns, Lorilee Craker, Tracy Groot and Alison Hodgson. My publishing team: editors Amy Nemecek, Julie Schwab, McKenna Walter and graphic designers David Frees and Calli Mueller. And most of all, thanks to my husband, Dave Beach, writer and counselor, who daily graces my life with his profound spirit.

INTRODUCTION

CREATIVE JUICES AND ITS MOVING PARTS

Creative soul care. Process. Story craft. These three are the moving parts of the writing life.

Soul is Central Station for the writer's heart and mind, where fear or perfectionism or resistance may halt outgoing trains.

Process is creating a strategy, a game plan, a routine that acts like scaffolding that holds the worker high against the skyscraper to wash the windows, to do the job.

Story craft is the construction of the right angles, the building of the story, its walls, flooring and roof, its wiring, plumbing.

Throughout *Creative Juices,* explanations, examples and exercises support these three moving parts. This pedagogically-deft approach is a must in a supplemental text, so writers can learn to cultivate healthy creative habits and strong craft to foster long-term writing viability.

CREATIVE JUICES AS SNACKABLE CONTENT

An NPR program chatted about the change TV broadcast stations planned to make in shortening commercials to compete with streaming networks. This new emphasis, a Web-driven change called "snackable content," loves all things short and all things story.

Creative Juices is snackable content. It offers short, readable tidbits to energize fiction and nonfiction writers.

TWENTY-FIRST-CENTURY CRAFT

Craft rules, like punctuation rules, bend and change. We stand in a river after all.

Careful readers have noticed these changes. Some have dropped the Oxford comma. Everything's shorter and faster. This means quicker openings (often *in medias res,* that is, in the middle of the action), shorter total lengths (even most adult novels have dropped 20,000 words), heaps more white space and action beats instead of dialogue tags. In nonfiction, we notice the warm embrace of story craft techniques even in hard news.

Much reading in college English classes draws from twentieth-century literature or earlier. Thus, often a literature class offers a close study of story craft that, no matter how beautiful, is quite frankly dated. That said, the likes of Flannery O'Connor (think "Revelation"), Eudora Welty and John Updike can still teach us writers much.

As a professor, writer and coach, I draw from a stocked pantry to offer this writing book. As a professor, I've clocked over twenty-five years as a full-time instructor. As a writer, I straddle nonfiction with my MA in journalism from Wheaton College and fiction with my MFA. My work appears in newspapers, literary journals and books. As a writing coach, I studied under Dr. Eric Maisel, a nationally known creativity coach. I have led creativity groups and classes in Seattle and Grand Rapids since 1999 and am a certified spiritual director.

Perhaps my best recommendation, however, is this: I love writing. Me thinks you do as well.

"Our stories tell us who we are, why we are here and what we can do. They give us our best answers to all of life's big questions, and to most of the small ones as well."

DANIEL TAYLOR

SECTION I

Soul is Central Station for the writer's heart and mind, where fear or perfectionism or resistance may halt outgoing trains.

Chapter 1

SOUL TUNING

He stood tall, rangy, big-boned. A tether lassoed his hair into a ponytail. Hells Angels motorcyclist? His big paw could easily cup a helmet, but this man was no biker. This man was none other than exquisite wordsmith and profound storyteller Walter Wangerin Jr.

The Book of the Dun Cow. The Book of Sorrows. Miz Lil. His marrow-of-the-bone, award-winning works wrestled for my attention. And now Wangerin was about to give me the gift of a word—not just any word, but a guiding word for writers.

To find this word, a word now dead in our spoken language, Wangerin had opened an antiquated dictionary and blew from its pages the dust of centuries. There he had found the call-affirming word: "scop."[1]

This long-buried word sounds like "shope"—and now how I'll spell it is "schope."

The word "schope" named a difficult career in ancient Greece, a career that would push someone against the fiber of heart and verve. After a war, the schope crossed the battlefield to record what had happened. Who had won? Who lost? Who died—or lived? This early reporter saw it all—and had to see. The schope's effort to see and record named the event for the surrounding community and, thus, created understanding.

The word's meaning then drifted. In the Middle Ages, schope referred to the bard, the courtier who put into words and music the stories of the kingdom and its people. Eventually, schope became a word we commonly use today: "shape."

We writers are shapers. We shape life into story. Maybe the story of our day. Maybe the story of another day. Maybe the story of what is or the story of what can be. By doing so, we serve. Perhaps our writing is the way we enact our being, the way we stand in the world and love.

SEEING THINGS: ONE WRITER'S CALL

The weathered post wore a sculpted head, its old curves elegant. It rose from the sand and framed the right edge of the vista that spread beyond a dune to encompass Lake Huron.

I was a teen living near the lake and loved to walk along shore to think. Up the dune I'd scramble, my feet sunk in sand. At the crest, I'd pause to gape. The sweep of sand. The horizon stretch of blue-silver. The post anchoring the near corner of the picture I always imagined snapping.

Then one day I climbed the dune and—no post. Gone. Disappointment surged through me. Later, when I lamented to my family about it, they responded, "What post?"

The post became my symbol for that Something About Me—that part of me that noticed things others didn't. My physical eye saw details like the post; my inner eye saw other details—emotional currents, nonverbal signals.

This seeing, at times, propelled me into isolation. It wasn't an attribute I prized. My pain echoed in the words of Lara, the character from the Russian novel *Doctor Zhivago*. For Lara asks, "Why is it my fate to see everything and take it all to heart?"[2]

As teachers encouraged me to write—to record what my seeing revealed—I began to value this trait a little. Maybe it was a gift. I even began encountering ways of understanding this seeing.

Catherine Marshall's novel, *Christy,* taught me that God might be the One asking me to see. Christy's mentor explains, "God has been gently, steadily prying the little girl's hands off the little girl's eyes."[3] This idea electrified me. I understood. Be willing to see.

Other reading confirmed this seeing, this bearing witness, as important. Russian poet Anna Akhmatova showed its importance in this account:

In the terrible years of the Yezhov terror, I spent seventeen months waiting in line outside the prison in Leningrad. One day somebody in the crowd identified me. Standing behind me was a woman, with lips blue from the cold, who had, of course, never heard me called by name before. Now she started out of her torpor common to us all and asked me in a whisper, (everyone whispered there):

"Can you describe this?"
And I said, "I can."
Then something like a smile passed fleetingly over what had once been her face.[4]

A recognized poet—her power to see and to name—stirred a desperate woman's hope. My seeing was a gift. I would try. I would try to look around me, to be the one to see.

"Writing . . . can get you to start paying attention,
can help you soften, can wake you up."
ANNE LAMOTT,
BIRD BY BIRD

BRAIN MATTER

Write It: You may or may not call yourself a writer, and yet you hold this book. So, what prods you to write? Or you may feel a sense of calling. If so, describe it.

Ponder It: What is your writing story? When did you become aware of this vocational conviction?

Chapter 2

CREATIVE SOUL CARE

You and I have creative arteries as assuredly as we have physical arteries that carry a swish of oxygenated blood to and fro. Like our physical arteries, these creative arteries can be healthy and strong, or they can be weakened and diseased. We decide the health of our creative arteries. Our habits, choices and self-talk can cause peripheral artery disease (PAD) in our creative souls.

Unfortunately, as a writer, I nearly succumbed to creative PAD. The combination of my first years of college instructing and my unmanaged perfectionism constricted my creative arteries. Writing grew more and more difficult. Soon my creative flow trickled. I stopped writing. Then someone gave me Julia Cameron's *The Artist's Way*.

Cameron was an early voice in the creativity movement, what editor Lil Copan calls "creative formation."[1] Cameron and now many others suggest that certain practices support creativity well. (Religious folks may see an echo here of spiritual formation or spiritual disciplines: solitude, meditation, prayer, celebration, etc.)

Take time to play. Fill the well, she said. And I began to realize how my putting "play" at the end of my list made sure of only one thing: I never played.

Actively heal your wounds, Cameron added, suggesting how. So, I practiced healing habits. I drew caricatures of people who had been cruel. I journaled.

She even challenged me to explore my notions of God and creativity. Did I believe that God saw my creativity—especially fiction writing—as frivolous? Maybe my fiction mattered, but was simply of lesser value in the scheme of things. Well, then again, maybe my fiction did matter.

As I did my soul work, health returned to my creative arteries. My creativity flowed once more.

BRAIN MATTER

Rate It: On a scale of 0 to 5 with 5 being excellent, rate your creative flow. What do you notice?

SOUL DROUGHT & SOUL CARE

Lexington Reservoir was a sheet of silver tucked high into the Santa Clara foothills. I knew this California lake well. I had traveled its waters, after all, when Dad packed me into the little El Toro and pushed off from shore. I knew it from other days when State Route 17 carried us near it in our red VW bus. From the backseat, I would stare, mesmerized by its shimmer.

Then 1976 arrived.

For those of us who recall that time, we remember it as a year that ushered in many bicentennial celebrations. That year also ushered in a drought that changed how Californians did water.

Before the drought, Lexington had worn a thin brown belt, shoreline really, that attached its silver to the curve of hill and the shrub trees above it.

Then during 1976, the change I witnessed worried me. The thin belt grew wider and wider and wider as the lake succumbed. Shimmery silver turned silver-brown then darkened further to mud-brown before mud-brown dried alarmingly to cracked-brown. Dead fish soon gave way to bone.

I no longer knew my lake.

Our habits lower in the valley—in the city of San Jose—changed. Restaurants stopped serving water. We turned off faucets and showers. Dad stopped watering his lawn. We changed. Even today, although I live in a state known for its water, I can't bear to powerwash anything.

Our souls that may shimmer like a silver lake can succumb to drought, too. Overwork? Perfectionism? Lousy boundaries? These things can shrink the expanse of our souls like the drought of 1976 shrunk Lexington.

What are some creative soul care principles to keep ourselves from cracking with drought?

SOUL VITAMIN #1: FILL THE WELL

Like water management systems allotting water for Lexington or like carefully filling our canteens before crossing the desert, the notion of "filling the well" shows up often in talks on creative care.[2]

We need to do things, say creativity coaches, that pour back into us. If certain actions like shopping or doing math deplete you, find some activities that do the opposite—that give you a sense of spiritual limberness, rest or energy.

These activities fill me:
1. Exercise
2. Solitude
3. Scrapbooking or painting

BRAIN MATTER

List It: List five activities that fill you.

SOUL VITAMIN #2: PLAY

Zane Grey, a prolific storyteller whose eighty nine novels sold over forty million copies, learned about the importance of play the day he learned about fishing.

As a boy, his parents disapproved of those who fished; it offended their work ethic. But Grey fell in love with rivers and fish and the great outdoors, and when he met Old Muddy Miser, he learned an invaluable lesson:

> You must make fishing a study, a labor of love, no matter what your vocation will be. You must make time for your fishing. Whatever you do, you will do it all the better for the time and thought you give fishing.[3]

Old Muddy Miser's words allowed Grey to put play higher on his to-do list than his parents would have permitted, and through it, Grey found that there was no shame in loving and doing an activity that didn't seem to gain him much in the world of adult economy.

Why is an activity like fishing not a waste of time? Why might such things, in fact, be vital for us creatives?

Fishing or walking or painting or tinkering "fiddles" with your creative dials, says *Eat, Pray, Love* author Elizabeth Gilbert in *Big Magic*.[4] It's about opening our minds through creativity. It's not about performance or perfectionism. Thus, when novelist Tracy Groot gets tangled on a plot, she knits.

Even Einstein recognized the value of giving ourselves downtime. He names this "combinatory play."[5] We who get too good at adulting need to *let* ourselves play.

BRAIN MATTER

Apply It: How do you fiddle with your creative dials?

> "Rest is not idleness, and to lie sometimes on the grass under trees on a summer's day, listening to the murmur of the water, or watching the clouds float across the sky, is by no means a waste of time."
> JOHN LUBBOCK

SOUL VITAMIN #3: IDLE BRAIN TIME

Neuroscience rebuffs long-held prejudices against idleness and play. In *Autopilot: The Art & Science of Doing Nothing,* scientist and engineer Andrew Smart explains that focus actually suppresses our hippocampus and medial prefrontal cortex.[6] This means that when we focus, we decrease blood flow and oxygen to our brains. But when we "space out"—yes, daydream—blood and oxygen supercharge those parts of our brain. Idle brain time refuels the Default Mode Network (DMN).

How important is our DMN?

This network gives us our "aha moments." Consider how vital ideas are in creative work. So, if we as writers require such moments, how can we have healthy DMN?

1. Allow yourself time where you stare off into space, nap, walk, paint a wall or shovel manure.
2. Give yourself a union break, a sabbath and/or a good night's sleep.
3. Cultivate solitude.

INTEGRATIVE SOUL CARE: JOURNALING

Journal? I grumbled. *Me?*

I was stuck. My subplots were knots where I needed lines. But how could I get going again? An answer haunted me: journal!

That old tool? I'd prefer a magic wand.

Of course, I knew journaling's benefits. Writing theorist Dr. Peter Elbow has long promoted prewriting exercises like brainstorming or listing. These approaches mimic how those from northern climates used to warm their cars in winter. You'd sit in place and idle the car.

Another expert, Dr. James Pennebaker, cites medical studies that connect health benefits like an improved immune system with expressive writing (i.e., journaling).[7] And Julia Cameron compares her tool Morning Pages—again, journaling—to a spiritual alignment.[8]

Me, journal? For figuring subplots? I eyed my resistance. "You should journal every day," a nagging voice said.

Bah humbug!

I overrode this resistance, though, and reached for a pen. I dug out my long-neglected notebook and wrote one paragraph. Something within me loosened. An idea arrived and brought along an idea's best friend, energy. The knot slipped loose. I opened my manuscript document and wrote.

You, too, may find yourself groaning over the idea of journaling. It's common. For more than one reason. Most of us have had a finger waved at us: You have to write every day. You have to journal every day. These commands may be fodder for shame or resistance. We want to journal—kind of. But we don't act. Shame builds plaque on our creative arteries.

Here's where our choice can be our friend. We can choose. We can choose to journal and to care for our creative souls. We also can avoid the "every day" rule as well by setting a smaller goal like journaling once a week.

Journaling is like an old friend who's seen us at our best—and our worst. It's a place to park our fears, our worries, our self-doubts. And like a friend, it can diffuse our feelings and show us new action plans.

While journaling tends our creative soul, it gives us an extra bonus: journaling builds our writing muscle.

BRAIN MATTER

Write It:
1. Describe your experience with journaling. How does it benefit you?
2. Does thinking about journaling provoke your resistance? If yes, explain the trigger. What might be beneath it?

ANTIDOTES TO WRITING BLOWS

The creative life and the writing business, which humorist Alison Hodgson (*The Pug List*) refers to as "this horrible business," sometimes compares to entering a boxing ring and letting your face be pummeled.

But this time? It's your heart.

Several writing instructors warned me of this dreadful fact: on average, 78 percent of our writing will get a no. Not a quarter. Not half. Three-fourths of our writing. No after no hurts. It is, in fact, traumatic.

The writing journey bruises and breaks us. Our ego. Our outlook. Our sense of calling. Our heart. Our definition of life and God—and how we think God should show up for us. So, for our writing journey, we need to pack a first aid kit. And we need it on hand at moment's notice.

Writing Blows First Aid Kit

1. Journal your laments and pain.
2. Up self-nurturing.
3. Pray (voicing laments and/or a whole lot of anger).
4. Talk to friends who understand.
5. Write.

By using these antidotes, we can heal and return to the ring. My writing pals and I give each other twenty-four hours for full-throttle mourning, and then we say, "Back to work."

BRAIN MATTER

Write It: Cameron recommends journaling through this wound-probing tool, "Blasting through Blocks."[9]

1. Create a list of your resentments or frustrations about this project.
2. List the fears this work may trigger. (e.g., I'm afraid my novel will be trite.)
3. What other fears do you have? Explore deeply.
4. What do you gain by not doing this project? (e.g., I can stay hidden and never put my stuff out there for comment.)

HEALING: PROBE THE WOUNDS

She had that fair skin of a redhead. As the twenty-six-year-old graduate student sat across from me for our first coaching session, her skin revealed much. She blushed before tears began to trickle. She started then to explain her emotion.

Ten years ago, she said, her high school teacher was handing back essays and called to her from across the room, "You are the worst writer I've ever had."

I stared. No wonder this student had tears.

"After that, I couldn't write." Shame burned in her face. "I used to write all the time. Poetry. Song lyrics. And now each time it's a struggle."

Of course. False shame had soldered shut her creative artery. This writer needed to do her soul work. She needed to probe the wound. Would she write a letter from her twenty-six-year-old self to that sixteen-year-old self about that terrible moment? She needed to stand against her teacher's destructive words and spirit.

The next time we met, I asked her if she had written her letter. She shook her head no. She hadn't.

"What do you think is stopping you?"

"It's hard."

To return into that moment would require great courage. Who'd want to? As her coach, though, I hoped. Would she choose to heal? Would she probe the wound?

At our next appointment, she arrived wearing a very different countenance. She beamed. "I did it. It helped!"

She got how wrong the teacher had been. She got what had happened to her in that moment. She got the false shame that had infected her creativity. By opening the wound, by doing some tending, she could heal.

A year later, she approached me, our times of meeting long finished. No flush slid up and into her face. No tears slid down.

"I'm writing now. I'm writing poetry again."

By doing her soul work and probing her wound, this young woman found the freedom to write.

BRAIN MATTER

Write It: Write a letter from your imagined eighty-year-old self to the present you. Let this older self speak into any disappointment, hurt, fear, anger that you feel about your writing. What writing advice does this older self offer?[10]

Perfectionism

Those who are perfectionistic tend to be among the top students or employees. Often these creatives, who accomplish tasks with frenetic energy—not true, quiet strength—have been positively rewarded for what may kill them in the end.

Perfectionism is *lethal* to creativity.

Perfectionism hardens our creative arteries. Which means long-term perfectionism has unforeseen consequences that we may not experience early on. Perfectionism requires deep soul work and important self-coaching. It's soul war.

According to Elizabeth Scott's "Perfectionistic Traits: Do They Sound Familiar?" certain behavioral clues show that we may be tending toward perfectionism:

- Procrastination or not ever starting
- Never finishing a project
- Angry or highly anxious core
- Highly critical of self and others
- Defensiveness over quality
- Unrealistic expectations[11]

But even the most hardened perfectionist can change—little by little, choice by choice.

Managing Perfectionism

Tool #1
To keep from overworking, set a time limit on how long you'll work on a project.

Tool #2
Explore through counseling what core emotion or wound drives your perfectionism.

Tool #3
Life coaches use the tool "Bull's Eye" to help clients manage perfectionism. This tool invites us to create a wider ring of acceptable outcomes, which may alleviate anxiety.

1. What would be the ideal level of accomplishment for this project? (e.g., My writing would be the level of Tolstoy's and would become an instant *New York Times* bestseller with a movie starring George Clooney.)
2. What range below my ideal is still acceptable? (e.g., I'd finish a strong novel manuscript and begin to market it.)
3. What falls below my level of acceptability?[12] (e.g., I wouldn't ever finish drafting my novel.)

> "Perfectionism is a mean, frozen
> form of idealism...."
> Anne Lamott,
> Bird by Bird

Procrastination:
The Good, the Bad and the Ugly

Teachers, parents, pastors and many other categories of adults believed years ago that procrastination signaled sloth—that is, laziness. Post–creativity movement, though, procrastination is seen as a strategy that gets someone what they want—or a sign of fear or performance anxiety.

And now, we also believe that for some, what may be mistaken as negative procrastination is an incubation time—a legitimate time of pondering the topic. This type of writer is doing the work. We just don't see it. They're thinking, musing, meditating; in fact, they're busy at it.

So, think about this: what lets us know whether or not our strategy is working? The quality of the end product, right?

Someone who habitually misses deadlines or doesn't allow time for sufficient revision is likely in the category of procrastination as a self-sabotaging strategy. Someone who is incubating can submit on-time quality work.

SELF-SABOTAGE

Imagine that initial contact for a first date—and the terror that accompanies this little question: do you like me enough to go out with me?

The Tom Hanks–Meg Ryan movie *Sleepless in Seattle* shows the stress a widower suffers when, after his wife's death, he calls for that first, post-marriage date. Character Sam Baldwin (Hanks) paces around the phone before suddenly grabbing it, jabbing the digits and talking rapidly. Once the girl says yes, he collapses into his chair. The guy's exhausted.[13]

St. Paul describes it well: half of me does and half of me doesn't.[14] I work against myself. We can be our worst enemy. Ambivalence divides us. Our desires divide us. Actions that feel risky flood us with ambivalence. *I should contact that editor. No . . . wait. I shouldn't.*

While part of you works to write, the other half of you will work against your writing. Get onto yourself. How do you self-sabotage? What's your preferred flavor?

Self-sabotage takes on many masks:

- Describing in detail a new idea—when you need to let it remain in silence and incubate
- Setting small goals and not doing them
- Missing times of celebrating your successes small and large
- Not letting yourself write

What other actions might have self-sabotage at their root? Another might be not letting yourself finish a project by inflating all that must be done.

> "Creative U-turns are always born
> from fear—fear from
> success or fear of failure."
> JULIA CAMERON,
> THE ARTIST'S WAY

The Creative U-turn is something to watch for, too. This move, aptly named by Julia Cameron, happens when we love an idea or action step, are happily moving toward it and then—*poof!*—without reason, turn cold.[15] On a wedding day it's called "cold feet." Journaling or talking to friends can ease this symptom of fear.

Recovering alcoholics let an important policy guide them as they work hard to change their behavior: HALT. This acronym says that when we're hungry, angry, lonely and/or tired, we're vulnerable and that we need to choose and act with care.

Appropriate self-care can help ward off our propensity toward sabotage. Even doing something as simple as positive reinforcement—rewarding ourselves—can strengthen us.

BRAIN MATTER

Write It: Describe a time when you pulled a Creative U-turn.

NEGATIVE SENTIMENT OVERRIDE
The art of closing the door to a new opportunity before you ever need to walk through it by imagining only negative outcomes.
Cure: Stop it.

GOLD STARS AND OTHER REWARDS

Miss Sorenson had me at "Hello, class, welcome to fourth grade." She was blond and petite and beauty-contest beautiful. And she was the kinder of the two fourth-grade teachers—not like that other one who had once rapped my knuckles at recess. Even more important to my nine-year-old values were Miss Sorenson's suede pumps. They were the color of purple crayons.

Miss Sorenson had me another way: her glittering gold stars. Like many teachers, she topped good homework with these five-pointed stickers. Was her approach original? No. Thousands of elementary teachers stick gold stars on noteworthy assignments. Why? Because it works. Think B. F. Skinner and the psychology of operant conditioning.

Recently, I purchased a packet of gold stars from Spring Grove Variety, the dime store in town. Now these stars glimmer on scene cards that hold good writing. Each time I award myself a star, positive memory surges through me. Fourth-grade accomplishments. Miss Sorenson. Purple suede shoes. *Well done,* I think. *You did it!*

My reward system isn't limited, however, to literal gold stars. An ice cream cone, a walk, a day off will do. Giving myself a gold star helps quiet the negative Critic's voice and keeps me heartened. I achieved my goal—and I notice.

So, what will be my gold star for getting a book published? I have no doubt. Purple suede shoes.

BRAIN MATTER

List It: What are five of your rewards? (e.g., taking a nap.)

CHERISHING THE WRITING LIFE

Contributed by Dr. Dave Beach[16]

If we could see our own lives, our own stories, at a deeper level, perhaps we would see the thumbprint of a loving God all around us; and we would love or even cherish our creative life, our writing life.

But what specifically do we mean by "love"? If we follow this word's dynamic meanings, we'll encounter meanings that fail. Love can be synonymous with strong words like "idolize" or "worship," but love also can mean milder words like "prefer" or "fancy."

I prefer the British meaning of the word "cherish": "to love, protect and care for someone or something that is important to you."

I cherish my wife, my daughter, my friends, my freedom, my solitude, my quiet time for writing, my books, my library, (possibly my MacBook), but do I cherish—"love, protect and care for because it is important to me"—the writing life?

Gregory Ciotti says, "The love we have for our art is perhaps one of the most important qualities of creativity. The love—not for outcomes, but for the process—that lets us find out what's inside of us, to remind us why we're alive, to create value for others, is as precious as time and close friends."[17]

What if I treated my love for writing as a clue to how I love other people and things? What if I could resolve and vow to love the writing life until death parts us? Forever, for always, and no matter what? What would happen? What would change?

SECTION II

Process is creating a strategy,
a game plan, a routine that acts
like scaffolding holding
the worker high against
the skyscraper to wash the
windows, to do the job.

Chapter 3
PROCESS PERFORMANCE

If your writing process—the collection of your strategies, rituals, habits, approaches to writing—were a car, what kind would it be?

- A rusted-out beater that's missing one tire
- A tiny sedan carrying five king-sized mattresses
- A sleek and powerful Corvette

Your process is the vehicle that gets you from Point A to Point B. What are the many things you do—or don't do—to get the job done? Some writers procrastinate, which can be negative—or positive as we read in Chapter 2. Some eat a handful of chocolate chips, while others launder their whites—or floss. Some outline; others plunge into drafting.

Your process matters. (But let's be clear: there isn't *one* perfect process.) That said, being a writer isn't only having verbal talent. Being a writer includes intentionally forming and practicing habits that get the writing done.

The world of sports underscores the value of strategies in having common "plays." Football uses the sweep, the quarterback sneak or the end around. Why? These plays—these strategies—get the job done.

Dr. Peter Elbow revolutionized notions about the process of writing when he broke writing into game plays: planning, drafting and revising. Each category holds multiple strategies. Here are some common ones:

Planning Tools: list, brainstorm, outline, map, bracket

Drafting Tools: start where the idea is clear, draft quickly, avoid editing, block infamous squiggly grammar lines, use symbol or caps for reminders

Revising Tools: use a cooldown, have a friend read, print hard copy, storyboard with stick-it notes, hire a professional editor, use a revision agenda, read aloud

Two types of at-risk writers who especially need to tend their process are the perfectionistic writer and the fearful writer. These writers are often riddled with the Critic, that negative voice in our head. The Critic will make enormous damning statements about our efforts like "This is no good" or "You're not a writer."

The good news? We have many tools to use; having many tools sets any craftsperson up for success. The catch? We have to make choices—use our formidable will—to employ them. And when we fail, which we will, we must forgive ourselves and continue forward.

Consider letting your process be flexible and dynamic, not stiff or static. Think of athletes and what aids them best: limber muscles.

Depending on the writing task's purpose and length, and as we ourselves move through developmental stages, our process needs to adapt. Trying new practices widens and enlarges us while solidifying our habits.

Tinker with your process by forming small commitments. New habits can feel strange. Expect that. To form new habits, we have to practice the new to get beyond the inevitable alien feel. Develop a combination of a few process tools and try them for several projects.

BRAIN MATTER

Write It: To explore your process, record your answers. Your goal is to explore which areas of your process help you get the job done and which areas don't.

1. Describe how you begin a writing project. Do you start immediately or delay? What planning tools do you use? What habits do you notice?
2. If you delay or procrastinate, do you use the delay to noodle or incubate your idea (which is positive action), or do you simply delay to avoid the task?
3. Describe how you approach the drafting stage. What tools do you use? What habits?
4. Describe your revision stage. What tools do you employ? Do you have a friend read it? How do you edit and proofread?
5. Which stage (planning, drafting, revising) is easiest for you? Why? Toughest? Explain.

PROJECT MANAGEMENT & GLITCHES

And while we're talking cars, how did the American car maker Henry Ford get that showy house in Grosse Point Woods, Michigan, that the public now pays to enter? In part, Ford used a process, a system, an effective game plan called the "assembly line." Today this strategy is cousin to what's now known as "project management."

From Pixar to Apple, corporations care deeply about project management: how do you get employees to start, continue and finish a project? Implied in this concern, of course, is how difficult it can be for us to undertake projects. Pixar president Ed Catmull states what he sees as common:

> People who take on complicated creative projects become lost at some point in the process. It is the nature of things—in order to create, you must internalize and almost become the project for a while, and that near-fusing with the project is an essential part of its emergence. But it is also confusing.[1]

Notice how Catmull acknowledges that losing our way in a project—becoming confused—is normal.

The other arts share similar process challenges. Elizabeth Ivy Hawkins, an artist-writer and coach, blogs about what she notices about her painting process and glitches:

> Step one is priming the surface and starting to build shape in thin painted layers. These are my scaffolding, the structure that I build the work around. The first two layers are on two new paintings, and they will take about 24 hours to dry.
>
> I hate this part. It is surprising for me to say it, and it's the truth. I am thrilled that I painted, once a form takes on a life and a being all its own. But I hate the icky directionless. I hate the trial and error. I want to skip to the end. Today, I observe the discontent in me.
>
> When you make something original, sooner or later you run into resistance. Fear of failure, comparison and underlying anxiety are my most common forms.[2]

This artist-writer articulates her resistance to the middle stage where she flounders in feeling directionless.

You and I—whether we are painters, writers or business people—have process glitches. We habitually get stuck at the same place in many of our projects—either the project's start, middle or end. This next exercise examines how you experience the different process stages.

BRAIN MATTER

Write It: In terms of beginning a project, moving through its middle stage and finishing, consider the following:

1. Which stage do you tend to lose energy—beginning, middle or end? Where do you lose interest or feel most anxious?
2. In which stage or stages is your energy high?

Find It: To explore strategies available for overcoming process glitches, google your weakest. Record helpful suggestions.

- How to start a writing project
- How to keep going in the middle of a project
- How to finish a writing project

> "When I face the desolate impossibility of writing five hundred pages, a sick sense of failure falls on me, and I know I can never do it. Then gradually, I write one page and then another. One day's work is all I can permit myself to contemplate."
> JOHN STEINBECK

SMALL GOALS

Formulating and committing to small goals can ensure our writing efforts. Devotees of *Bird by Bird* by Anne Lamott will recall the echo of this approach. This writing guru says that we become "immobilized by the hugeness of the task ahead."[3] So, to prevent this typical response, Lamott suggests writing "one small scene, one memory, one exchange."[4]

In other words, break the project down.

For example, I don't sit down to write a 95,000-word novel. I sit down and write one scene. We're talking about 300 words—which many writers can do as a crappy first draft while the veggie omelet cooks.

A possible small goal for someone returning to writing is the goal of writing for fifteen minutes two or three times a week. We can see how similar this is to a return to exercising. We don't run a marathon on the first day.

On the other hand, for someone with toned writing muscles, setting a more challenging goal will foster new growth. Author James Scott Bell challenges writers to draft 350 words, six days a week.[5]

So, think small . . . for a time.

BRAIN MATTER

Consider It: What would be a small goal that you can set for yourself? A larger one? Practice one goal for two weeks. What do you notice?

Write It: We've examined process tools like listing or taking a cooldown, and you've googled project management strategies. What tool or strategy interests you? What growth would you like to see—and work toward—in your process?

Process Challenge: Commit to practicing one strategy for two projects. Then examine its impact on your process.

PLOTTERS, PANTSERS & THE GOLDEN MEAN

New York Times bestselling author Elizabeth George wishes that she had done process differently during the early years of her very successful writing career. "I wish that I had known back then that a mastery of process would lead to a product. Then I probably wouldn't have found it so frightening to write."[6]

George, whose British mysteries have been made into BBC productions, says she's a plotter. A plotter is someone who uses a range of planning tools, such as outlining, before drafting. George moves through planning techniques and even visits Britain to research before she drafts. Plotters generally want to see their way clear before starting.

On the other side are "pantsers" like novelist Steven James, who prefers to jump into fast-drafting his psychological thrillers. In *Story Trumps Structure*, James urges writers to dump outlines and, instead, to write "organically."

You can imagine how these two camps might quibble.

But what if we use tools to strengthen our weaknesses—whether we're a plotter or a pantser? For plotters, soften rigidity. For pantsers, improve organization.

Aristotle underscores this goal and calls it "the Golden Mean." This ancient philosopher suggested that the place of strength—or highest virtue—was between two extremes. Other philosophical thought might call this a "both/and" instead of an "either/or."

As a confirmed pantser, I create problems for myself when I skip planning and only draft. While I still don't use a formal outline before drafting, I have found softer plotter tools that pull me from my perch on the extreme pantser end. Now I list or brainstorm. I also use Fred White's Novel Draft Management Worksheet from *Where Do You Get Your Ideas?*[7] The point of White's worksheet is to summarize briefly each chapter of a novel—before the novel is written. The ease I had doing it for the first time surprised me, and it's been my guide ever since. This exercise pushes me toward the Golden Mean.

> ## PROCESS RIGIDITY
> Take your process temperature. If you're feeling highly resistant to exploring or trying process tools, be aware. If you want to write and aren't, be concerned.

Pantser Tools for Plotters

Pantser Steven James offers these "organic writing" tools in *Story Trumps Structure:*

- Explore the normal life of your protagonist—before the inciting incident.
- Take rabbit trails: go with a new idea. Try it.
- Draft the scenes you know you'll need.[8]

Plotter Tools for Pantsers

Mystery writer and plotter Elizabeth George offers these tools in *Write Away:*

- List your cast of characters: name, develop appearance, personality.
- Create a step outline: list ten to fifteen scenes and put in order.
- Draft a running plot outline, present-tense stream-of-consciousness.[9]

If our goal isn't achieving some mythic process, but merely improving our weaknesses, these small changes become manageable.

LOST DOGS & FIRST RESPONSES

Brother held my thirteen-year-old heart. In his paws. Brother, a Norwegian elkhound, was our best dog ever. His patience and kindness astounded my sister and me. If he found me crying, he would place his paw sympathetically on my arm.

So, did Brother ever surprise me that day we walked to the plum orchard behind our house, and I thought it a brilliant idea to unleash him. *Click.* Off Brother sprinted, his curled tail disappearing behind the brush. I called. I wailed. No Brother. Gone. Soon I scrambled to explain to Mom what I had done.

How we got him back, I don't recall. We did, though, and when Brother returned, so happy to see me, did I scold or spank him? I did *not*. Instead, I abided by the Golden Rule for Returned Dogs: Receive thy dog well.

I wrapped my arm around Brother's thick-furred neck and loved him. Why? Well, again we return to psychiatrist B. F. Skinner and his theory of positive reinforcement. Give praise for the behavior you want. Reward good behavior. This response makes sense for treating our dogs well.

Might rewarding good behavior also be an effective and helpful policy in handling our first drafts?

Writing can be hard. It challenges our soul issues like fear and perfectionism and self-protection. It challenges us, too, in craft issues from sentences to scene building. After we've finally sat down and written, how might we respond to that first draft? Do we reward ourselves for the good behavior of having written?

Yeah, no, right?

One man I coached—a successful businessperson—would always hear this after he wrote: "This is crap!" The voice was dismissive, chiding, shaming. Translated into a dog story, it'd be a very chilly reception for our returned pooch. The voice of the Critic shames.

Lamott, in *Bird by Bird,* encourages us to have very low expectations for our first draft. Let it be crap, she says.[10] In other words, do not expect perfection. In fact, receive what comes. Treat early drafts well with some old-fashioned positive reinforcement.

BRAIN MATTER

Write It: After you've drafted, which is loudest, your Muse praising you or the Critic blasting you? What is post-drafting like for you?

Chapter 4
PROCESS SUPPORT

What are ways we can support our process and give ourselves room to play? Check out these four approaches.

OVERWRITING: WORD GUSH

I was struggling. As I revised my novel manuscript, *The Surface of Water,* I was seeing only the edge of the co-protagonist's backstory. In her backstory, my character Trish is assaulted. But I didn't know the scene details—important clues to Trish's soul—yet.

Writer James Scott Bell gave me the tool, though, when my *Writer's Digest* magazine arrived. In Bell's article about revising, he said, "Gush out the words."[1]

This how-to tip especially resonated: "Open a new document and write for 5 to 10 minutes . . . concentrating only on creating as much new material as you can. Overwrite."[2]

Well, I thought, *what if I wrote the assault scene?*

Soon I had two pages of scene details. And what those two pages revealed! Trish now had specific triggers—the smell of peppermint from the perpetrator's breath and the Trentwood stairwell where it happened.

While this scene may not appear in my novel, the gems I discovered through overwriting—by letting my imagination focus and giving myself space to discover—serve the story.

BRAIN MATTER

Write It: Use Bell's method to word gush a problem scene.

RECORDING PUBLISHED COPY

Students learning musical composition are coached to copy down parts of famous scores. Why? Copying famous works reveals clever craft moves. Writers benefit from this technique as well.

Where in craft do you struggle? Description? Find a nugget from a favorite author and handwrite or type a few paragraphs. You'll feel language. You'll feel cadence. You'll feel style. You'll even feel such things as punctuation.

I used this technique for a key scene where my character Matthew Goodman experiences an epiphany. My scene lacked luster. So, I thumbed through an anthology until I found Eudora Welty's "The Death of the Traveling Salesman."

The story is a difficult read because Welty's nearly too clever for us. She uses an unreliable narrator, R. J. Bowman, someone who has lived cut off from others, a traveling shoe salesman whose relationships have been as deep as a puddle. And now he's very ill—influenza?—and doesn't know that he's in his last day of life.[3]

I returned to Bowman's epiphany, a gem, and typed each sentence. This slow task revealed Welty's craft moves. She used repetition, simile, metaphor—even an extended metaphor, an objective correlative. Then I returned to Matthew Goodman's epiphany and wrote. Something more beautiful emerged. My objective correlative deepened the moment, the intensity and allowed, I believe, the reader to experience more.

To see Welty's gem and how it improved my scene, see "Tricks of the Trade" in Chapter 13.

BRAIN MATTER

Record It: Find a favorite writer who can show you how to open a novel, describe a character or place, add power to an epiphany or make some other craft move. Pick a craft focus and then record a few paragraphs where the author pulls it off. What do you notice?

WRITING SPACE

"The physical universe doesn't lie."[4] These words offered at a coaching conference haunt me. Few places are these words truer than in what my writing room says to me on any given day.

No place to sit down? Too messy to work?

Whether we have a writing room or a separate house like John Steinbeck or a corner of a dorm room, our writing space tells us much.

First of all, do we give ourselves physical space to write? If not, why not?

Second, what's the space like?

I began noticing how my writing room alerted me to the condition of my creative soul. What told me this? Clutter. Often the more I write, the neater my space becomes. Would you have guessed this? Not me. But avoiding my writing results in an escalation of inner disorder. Outer disorder, too. Interesting, huh? What happens for you?

Clutter aside, other factors are important in our writing space. Does it contain the items that energize and inspire us?

Colors. I'm an old-fashioned girl, and my writing room reflects this vibe. The softest green shades the walls. White shelves anchor the sides of the room along with a robin-egg blue table and chair.

Special objects. Only treasures are allowed in my writing space. Pieces of Grandma Lackie's china. A copy of Elizabeth Gaskell's *North and South.* A Friesian model horse.

By giving myself writing space and then treating it like a place of value, I let me be in a supportive space that I love. Especially when I'm writing.

BRAIN MATTER

Write It:

1. Describe the space that you use for writing.
2. Describe your ideal writing space: colors, treasures, arrangement.
3. What can you modify about your current space to increase its sense as a place of value?

VISUAL AIDS

Corkboard fever. I have it in spades. Not one board. Not two. Not even three. No, four corkboards hang in my writing room, crammed with pictures.

These pictures guide the most basic ingredient of all in my fiction writing: specific details. They help me see my characters and settings.

It doesn't matter that now I've traveled with characters Trish and Pastor Goodman for ten years. The pictures still support me like training wheels on a kid's bike. They stabilize my mental image of each character's face, hair, hands, pose.

Details from pictures of a young Candice Bergen, the award-winning actress, saturate my descriptions: the square watch face, the low-slung ponytails, the sunglasses on her head. Another Bergen shot in warm sunlight is an extreme close-up where her fingers curl around her blowing hair. These pictures let me fully realize my character Esther, mother of co-protagonist Trish.

Another actor coached my ability to see Trish herself. I had clipped pictures of an Eddie Bauer model who, like Trish, had long blond hair. But then I saw the movie *Another Earth* with Brit Marling and I experienced a moment of realization. *Trish!* Dark, level brows, a steady and direct gaze. Marling lent a parcel of excellent details to bring Trish to life.

What of Matthew Goodman himself? Goodman needs good looks to survive a career involving broadcasted sermons. The face and hair of actor Bruce Greenwood fed my imagination. Greenwood, although now aged past my character, sports a boyish yet dignified appearance. How? The deep forehead, the thick hair, the wide-set eyes. Such details are the fodder that feeds my imagination—and awaken my readers' imagination.

Pinterest offers us writers endless virtual space to gather pictures for props, setting, characters that fortify our imagination. According to Tee Morris and Pip Ballantine in *Social Media for Writers,* an additional perk is the option to keep our boards hidden, if we wish, until we're ready to publish.[5]

So, virtual or real, corkboards offer us the space to gather pictures that fuel our writing.

BRAIN MATTER

Cork It: Collect pictures that serve you with details about your characters and setting. Build a digital or physical corkboard.

SECTION III

Story craft is the construction of the right angles, the building of the story, its walls and flooring and roof, its wiring, plumbing.

Chapter 5
STORY CRAFT FOUNDATION

Longtime nonfiction writer Larry Cheek, who wrote for national magazines like *Arizona Highways,* learned something of life and craft as he used his hands to build in his garage a thirteen-foot sailing dinghy.

His slow learning and adept noticing. His quiet, patient work along with his frustrations and discouragement. Letting his hands learn the feel of wood—when it was wet enough to bend or dry enough to glue. His hands learned; he learned. And over a year's time, his hands built his sailboat, *Far From Perfect,* that in full sail delivered him to Whidbey Island, ready to teach MFA-level writers about craft.

Cheek's woodworking lessons, recorded in *The Year of the Boat,* echo lessons about word working. Woodcraft teaches how to hone the lip of a piece of wood to fit with another, how to sand and smooth, so splinters will not ruin your next voyage. Story craft teaches how to listen so hard to words that you hear beneath them—their cadence, their musicality. How you use dialogue and plot and characterization. How you use words to describe, to bring to life the wonderful world of story.

SHOWING, SENSES AND SPECIFICS: THE FOUNDATION OF STORY CRAFT

Backhoes throttled as they scraped and scooped lawn to create a place for Cornerstone University's new science building. Days later, concrete trucks rumbled on-site, their mixing drums rotating. Soon, shuttling down their chutes came concrete. This mix of sand, rock, water and cement will brace the weight of a 29,500-square-foot building.

Showing and using the senses and specifics blend to make the concrete foundation for our stories.

Show, Don't Tell

The most foundational of story craft mottos is the familiar "Show, don't tell," which coaches us to let our readers experience a verbally constructed world. While maturing in story craft also matures our know-how of when to show and when to tell, we must first master showing. Showing reveals concrete details instead of merely offering labels.

Telling: She was old.

Showing: White hair waved across her head. [Description]

Telling: He was angry.

Showing: He clenched his fist. [Nonverbal action]

Showing is a toolbox with multiple story craft tools: action, description, dialogue, setting. Look for in-depth coverage of action and description in the next chapter.

BRAIN MATTER

Revise It: Turn the following two-sentence telling into showing.

The young woman was in the coffee shop. It was crowded.

The Senses

Using the senses, when possible, transforms imagined into real. Novelist and editor Vinita Hampton Wright warns, "Writers often include only one of the senses in their writing."[1] That one sense we rarely neglect is, of course, sight. But what about the other senses? Taste, touch, sound, smell—and even intuition?

The other senses enliven our world building. For example, what else would you hear in a Kansas barn in 1856—besides the whickering of the plow horse or its hooves shifting straw? The high notes of a barn swallow. The scampering scratch of mice. The swish of horsetail. The prairie wind humming high notes along the roofline. And what about the smells? Manure. That was easy. Musty straw. Leather soap and oil when we near the peg where the harness hangs. Sensory data is laden with a spider web of other attachments that begin to create stories within stories.

Pulitzer Prize winner Anthony Doerr fills the pages of his World War II novel, *All the Light We Cannot See,* with the different senses. For example, "Marie-Laure LeBlanc stands alone in her bedroom smelling a leaflet she cannot read. Sirens wail. . . . The windowpanes rattle in their housing."[2] What makes Doerr's use of the senses especially masterful is that his young character, Marie-Laure, is blind.

Another sense that we sometimes neglect is the sixth sense—whatever you want to call "vibes" or gut or intuition. Both nonfiction and fiction writers may have characters who listen to their gut—or the hair on the back of their necks. Maybe someone is hiking bear country and something within them urges them to look back.

Layering our writing with the senses—and avoiding the sight-only temptation—becomes easy as we practice brainstorming the senses.

> "Good writing is supposed to evoke sensation in the reader—not the fact that it is raining, but the feeling of being rained upon."
> E. L. DOCTOROW

BRAIN MATTER

Chart It I: Conveying data through the senses "evokes sensation in the reader," as Doctorow says. Brainstorming the senses, a form of intentional overwriting, asks us to create a chart and then list each of the five senses. Brainstorm the senses for this quote: the "feeling of being rained upon."

Chart It II: Apply brainstorming the senses to your story by charting each of the senses: sight, sound, taste, touch, smell and intuition.

Think of a scene to brainstorm:
1. Open a new document or handwrite, creating a column for each of the senses.
2. List three to five per column—or more. Think. Imagine. Fully realize your scene.

Specifics

Specific details heighten description. What I refer to as "specifics" others may call "concrete details" or "particularities." To understand moving from general to specific, let's meet the Ladder of Specificity:

- Life form
- Mammal

- Canine
- Dog
- Poodle
- Toy poodle

The phrase "life form" sounds more alien than dog-like, and with that general phrase, we certainly don't picture a wisp of dog, a toy poodle.

You and I normally pull our nouns from the fourth rung. We might talk about our cat or dog at home. While fine in casual speech, moving at least one rung down to heighten specificity adds color, connotation and control. We awaken our reader with specifics.

The web of attached meanings also lets us play with and deepen our scenes. Picture a thirty-year-old woman driving a Rolls Royce. What type of clothing is she wearing? What is her hairstyle like? Now notice how elements in your mental picture change when this thirty-year-old woman is driving an old Lumina. What is she wearing now? Hair? Shoes?

One rung down. That's all. I simply changed the type of car.

Memoirist Lorilee Craker makes good use of specifics and the senses in this scene from *Anne of Green Gables, My Daughter & Me.* Craker is in Seoul, South Korea, adopting her daughter, Phoebe:

> I was drawn to marts during our trip (not to mention the fact that they were a blast of frigid air in Seoul, which was draped in humidity like a wet sleeping bag). The cozy marts smelled cool and spicy, like green tea and ginseng, kimchi and sesame oil.[3]

Notice how the last line holds a host of specifics that radiate into our reading experience and our senses? The slightly musty smell of green tea. The sour smell of the cabbage dish kimchi. Craker's use of specifics snaps her scene into reality. Her readers visit Asia from the comfort of home.

Literary fiction writer Ian McEwan uses specifics beautifully in *Atonement.* In describing a female character, Cecilia, from viewpoint character Robbie Turner, a man who loves her, we see specifics at work: "A drop of water on her upper arm. . . . On her back, a mole half covered by a strap."[4] McEwan artfully serves his readers unique and specific details.

TRICKS OF THE TRADE

We needn't worry about choosing specificity while drafting. Remember Anne Lamott's motto: "Crappy first draft." But, by revising toward specifics, we strengthen our writing.

- Exterminate general words: bird to cardinal
- Use brand or proper names: soda to Coke
- Use numbers when possible: several to four

BRAIN MATTER

Revise It: Replace general words with specifics.

Every evening I go to my car to drive home. I snap on the radio and listen to music as I turn onto the highway.

Chapter 6
SHOWING TOOLS

In order to pour a foundation strong enough to build our readers' imaginations, we must master "Show, don't tell." Let's examine the two tools of action and description that help us ready the concrete mix of showing.

ACTION

Action shows. Our characters' actions—from gestures to posture to gait—reveal their souls. Actors know which actions reveal soul accurately and can teach us. Hawk subtle actions from films. Look for the slope of shoulder or the shape of a smile or the movement hands make.

Director-writer Ed Solomon uses character action in *Levity* to reveal the soul of newly released murderer Manuel Jordan, a man who can't forgive himself.[1] In an early scene, Manuel (Billy Bob Thorton) walks down a subway tunnel, a solitary man heading one direction while crowds move past in the opposite direction. Immediately, we know that he's out of step and unconnected. What shows me? Manuel walks against pedestrian flow. Action shows.

Solomon's full-circle ending cleverly returns Manuel to this same crowded tunnel. Now, though, having begun to forgive himself, he walks in step with others. This action assures viewers. Manuel will live.

> "The character will spring to life only when he is put to the test, when he is forced to make a decision and act."
>
> JAMES N. FREY

Like *Levity*, the short story "Escapes" by Ann Hood offers concluding action to show that the protagonists will flourish. Aunt Caryn and her niece, Jennifer, have been at odds. But now after a fierce conversation, we read: "The ferry arrives, and we move forward, toward it. Its steps are steep, and we have to link arms for the climb."[2]

This last line uses action to show. Life is tough, we understand it to say, but together Caryn and Jennifer can face it.

According to communication theorists, actions might include more than we expect:

- Kinesics: motion from our face to feet
- Voice: volume level, pace and quality
- Self-presentation: our clothing, props
- Proxemics: use of space[3]

As writers of both fiction and nonfiction, we work these categories to reveal our characters.

BRAIN MATTER

Write It: Using only nonverbal actions, show the response a character has when he or she, having just begun a new diet, arrives home to an empty house where a plate of steaming Tollhouse chocolate chip cookies awaits.

DESCRIPTION

Description shows. Description—sometimes brief, sometimes longer—lets us see the nonfictional or fictional character and setting. We begin watching imagination's movie. We're there. Description—with the help of specifics and the senses—reveals age, status, personality and motives.

Some writers dismiss description too quickly. Perhaps they remember as readers encountering what felt like endless (and maybe pointless) word after word of description. After all, twenty-first-century works tend to include less description. But description-adverse writers may be underestimating the importance and power of description. Descriptions are our bricks in world building and reality making.

In *Deepening Fiction,* Sarah Stone and Ron Nyren offer a continuum for understanding how much description to use. Maximalist description pegs a writer like Tom Clancy who is famous for long and detailed descriptions about submarine engines and the like.[4]

This Clancy maximalist description comes from political thriller *The Sum of All Fears:*

All three network morning news shows were originating from the Vatican. CNN was also there in force, as were NHK, BBC, and nearly every other network . . . all fighting for space in the grand piazza that sprawls before the church [began] in 1503 by Bramante, carried on by Raphael, Michelangelo, and Bernini.[5]

And this was only one-fourth of the paragraph. Notice, too, how Clancy breaks the norms for sentence length. Normal readability is around twenty words, but Clancy offers a detail-filled sentence twice that length.

On the other end of the continuum, we have minimalists who offer only brief description.[6] In *Tara Road,* Irish novelist Maeve Binchy opens a new scene with little world building, yet it's enough:

The phone rang in the sunny kitchen where Ria was busy making her scrapbook of Things to Do for when the children arrived.[7]

We aren't told the colors of the kitchen. We aren't told its type of flooring or appliances, but we see enough.

> "Description is not . . . 'all that flowery stuff.' Or, if description is the flowering, it is also the root and stem of effective writing."
>
> REBECCA MCCLANAHAN,
> WORD PAINTING

Artful or literary fiction tends toward maximalist description while commercial fiction uses less. While there's increased demand for brevity and white space, the advent of creative nonfiction has renewed love for fine word-smithing in popular works. So much so, that premier agent Donald Maass says that twenty-first-century writers ought to focus energy on mastering artful writing.[8]

BRAIN MATTER

Consider It: As you ponder this continuum of description, maximalist to minimalist, where do you peg your writing?

Fastdraft It: Write a scene with the opposite amount of description that you normally use. What do you notice?

TRICKS OF THE TRADE

An effective writer, whether a maximalist or minimalist, carefully manages description in these two areas:

1. Placing description in key spots;
2. Using a process in drafting description.

Placement of Description

Since part of our task is to create that movie image in our readers' minds, we must establish the who and the where. Otherwise our readers will begin imagining without our guidance—and may be jolted out of the "dream" when they read that our protagonist's neighbor isn't a short blonde, but is instead a six-foot-tall female bodybuilder.

During revision, check every new scene to see if early on a sentence or two describes the setting. Where are we now? This is called "setting the scene." Novelist Steven James explains that setting the scene "orients the reader."[9] Also check the pages where new characters arrive. Each one needs an immediate description—however brief.

A helpful move: add "setting the scene" to your revision checklist to aid world building. Being mindful during revision will guarantee the needed attention description requires.

Process of Description

A common worry we may have with description is knowing when too much is too much. But what if that worry—too early in our process—limits a goldmine discovery?

To allow plenty of room to discover and play, adopt a description process that lets you explore.

Drafting and initial revising:
- Word gush. Aim for the maximalist side. Overwrite.
- Brainstorm the senses.

Later revisions:
- Limit description to purpose and conciseness.
- Read aloud. This technique helps us catch many glitches, including wordiness.

Chapter 7

CHARACTERS ALIVE

A decade before William Goldman wrote *The Princess Bride,* he penned a bad-boy buddy screenplay called *Butch Cassidy and the Sundance Kid.* The prolific Goldman didn't know what he was doing, he says. Yet his script sold for more than any other Hollywood screenplay of its day. Goldman says, "Look, it's as if I knew what I was doing! The fact is that I had no idea. I was trying to tell this story that moved me . . . I had never written a movie. And all I had was the love of the two guys and the nuttiness of what they did."[1]

Goldman's characters had simply arrived, loosely based on two historical gunslingers. His love for Butch and Sundance and their antics led him to his story.

Have you ever experienced a character's arrival like that? Sometimes our story may start with our characters.

Listen to your characters. Focus. Let your characters be who they are. (You may feel a loss of control. Expect this. It's a good sign.) They may first appear like a shadow and then develop color and layers—the layers that will fix the needed verisimilitude, or believability.

> "Put simply:
> a character must
> be credible . . ."
> ROBERT MCKEE,
> STORY

APPEARANCE

The day I first met Dave, a thirty-six-year-old widower who had returned to college—the college where I taught—I assessed his appearance. His brown side-parted hair. His Abraham Lincoln cheekbones. His silver-blue eyes. The seriousness of his face told me that here was a man blistered by life. He intrigued me.

This outmost ring of Dave—his appearance—let me in on the inner rings as well—who this man was on the inside.

A character's appearance matters because of the hints it gives to the character's soul and history. Facial features, attitude of countenance, style (hair, clothes, props), height, weight, stance, teeth and fingernails whisper clues and contradictions about our characters.

Moving Beyond Stereotypes

Contributed by Martha Kay Salinas[2]

Have you ever noticed that movies with young male actors often have similar types of actors in the lead roles? They often have sensitive, well-defined, almost delicate features and large eyes. They're almost always white with really good hair that is usually straight and often blond or sandy brown.

Then there are the sidekicks: the fat kid, the Asian kid, the African American kid, the Mexican American kid, the kid with thick glasses, the brilliant nerd, the disabled kid and the kid with unruly curly hair.

This practice of casting a certain "look" in most lead roles is harmful in so many ways, but primarily in regard to setting up the sensitive white kid as the "standard." Most of us could look at cast photos before a movie is made and identify the lead character.

We shouldn't underestimate the emotional value of movies such as *Black Panther*. Can you imagine never seeing a heroic lead with your skin color? *Black Panther* brought in $1.344 billion dollars as of May 2018, which makes me hopeful that we'll be seeing more diversity in future superheroes.

Below are a few examples of lead characters, all of them white, most of them slight in stature with large eyes. Their sidekicks, or the secondary characters, are mostly white with single representations of the previously-mentioned groups.

For example, the television series *Stranger Things* has four white boys and one African American boy as the main characters. To the show's credit, the African American character comes from a more stable, well-to-do family than the other boys. Of course there are exceptions to the preponderance of white lead characters, but far too few.

Here are a few examples:

- *The Sandlot:* Scotty Smalls (Tom Guiry): straight sandy hair
- *Stand By Me:* Gordie Lachance (Wil Wheaton): straight sandy brown hair
- *Charlie and the Chocolate Factory:* Charlie Bucket (Peter Ostrum): wavy blond hair

- *Holes:* Stanley Yelnats (Shia LaBeouf): curly brown hair—the exception!
- *Star Wars,* Episode 4: Luke Skywalker (Mark Hamill): straight blond hair

Can you think of more examples or exceptions?

People come in an almost infinite variety of body types, nationalities, skin tones and races. Hair color and texture and eye color and shape vary widely. So why shouldn't lead characters fairly represent the population? If that were to happen, minority actors would portray approximately 23 percent of all lead characters. We have a long way to go.

Racism can be blatant or subtle, but it's harmful in any form or degree.

PROPS

Theater and film buffs may well love the notion of props: what the character carries, wears, travels in, and so on. You and I have props; we don't leave home without them. Mine include eyeglasses, Dansko shoes and a Buick that for a time had black duct tape on the passenger window.

We constantly assess and judge people by their props. Watches and cars and even dogs become status symbols or markers. Use this human habit to reveal your character and the world.

Ann Hood's short story "Escapes," previously mentioned for showing through action, uses character props well. Jennifer, the fourteen-year-old niece, wears a zillion shiny bracelets on her arms and long-sleeved shirts. These props function in two ways: they hide Jennifer's cutting and they later signal her deviant behavior of shoplifting.[3]

Remember what makes our readers fall into the story dream and be convinced of its reality: specific details. True for setting. True for characterization.

BRAIN MATTER

Write It:

1. Let your character look in a mirror. What does she or he see? Include it all: colors, shape, props.

2. List Ten: What are your character's props?

BACKSTORY

"Milo Rambaldi. Artist. Philosopher. Alchemist," says the narrator as the camera pans Leonardo da Vinci-like sketches. "His is a sixteenth-century voice that speaks to our own modern world. A man on a technological crusade."

The voice-over continues, "Born in 1440 in the sleepy town of Parma, Italy, Milo Giacomo Rambaldi was abandoned at birth on the doorstep of a Vespertine monastery."[4]

Sounds real, right? It's meant to. The catch, of course, to this *Alias* special feature, "The Legend of Rambaldi," is this: it's fiction. Rambaldi is a character.

The creators of this five-year TV series did their homework, though, and established a thorough backstory to Rambaldi. Birth year. Birthplace. The show creators even gave him a middle name.

We have the same job. For our characters, we must think through and decide who they are and what they're like—even their life offstage (or off-page).

BRAIN MATTER

Write It: Develop your character through these prompts:

- How old is your character? Birthdate? Place?
- What does your character drive? (And how?)
- What socioeconomic level is he or she? What about your character hints at this?
- How much education does your character have? What value does he or she place on it?
- What quirky habits might your character have?

Find It: Google a famous fictional character and read a Wikipedia biography. What details are given? What might they add to the personality of this character? Now write your own Wikipedia account of your character.

Emotions

Best bet in portraying character emotions? Be subtle. Show complexity through contradictory emotions, physical sensations and nonverbals.

Contradictory Emotions

We often herald the wedding day as the happiest day ever, yet even that day can be fraught with mixed emotions like joy and fear. "Here we go. Oh, wait! Do I really know him?" Our characters ought to be experiencing complex and contradictory emotions as well.

I recall a character moment I admired where an adult son—at his mom's funeral—wasn't crying. Instead, in this moment of deep grief, he sniffed loudly and quickly wiped his nose—as if ashamed of showing a normal grief response. Which, I believe, is often accurate. Think about how hidden we can be regarding our emotions. This character's shame over crying controlled him more—he felt it more deeply—than his sadness.

BRAIN MATTER

Consider It: What mix of emotions might your character or you, in the case of memoir, be confronting?

Physical Sensations

Nothing's easier—and perhaps more tempting—than telling emotions instead of showing them. Telling emotions sounds like this: "He was angry" or "She was happy." A better approach translates emotions into bodily sensations.

Weak: He was angry.
Better: Anger surged through him.
Best: Heat surged through him.

Notice how common the first one seems? Every writer uses this at times. But notice, too, how each example moves toward inner physical sensations? The final example lets us experience the emotion. Physical sensation is key.

Nonverbal Cues

The must-have *The Emotion Thesaurus: A Writer's Guide to Character Expression* lists physical signals for seventy-five emotions that range from "adoration" to "uncertainty."[5] If someone's lying, what happens to their eye contact? Their fingers? If someone's defeated, how does that affect their spine?

Think about how our nonverbal cues play such an enormous role in communication: head, facial muscles, eyes, eyebrows, nostrils, mouth, spine, shoulders, hands and so on.

> A fully alive character is never
> completely revealed, but is like an interior
> of a house glimpsed only through a window.
> A compelling part remains unseen."
> THAISA FRANK AND DOROTHY WALL,
> FINDING YOUR WRITER'S VOICE

BRAIN MATTER

Record It: List three physical sensations and three nonverbal cues for embarrassment.

DEEPENING CHARACTERIZATION

A successful photographer lives in a rundown house, but offers his guests very clean drinking glasses. A detective is sickened over blood. We round our characters by adding complexity and contrast.

Psychoanalyst Sigmund Freud likened us to the ubiquitous iceberg. In his Iceberg Theory of Personality, he asserted that like an iceberg, of which little shows, little of our inner motives and desires surface.[6]

A counselor friend keeps in his office a large multifaceted crystal. Its many facets remind him about human complexity as he sits with client after client. We all have many facets—some of them contradictory.

Like us, our characters are multifaceted crystals with contradictory and opposing desires and values.

BRAIN MATTER

Write It: Donald Maass, premier agent and craft guru, ramps up character complexity through these prompts in *The Breakout Novelist.*[7]

Focus on one of your characters and record:
1. What's something he or she wouldn't say?
2. What's something he or she wouldn't do?
3. What's something he or she wouldn't think?

Now, Maass says, where in your story might your character say, do or think what he or she would typically not? Record these possible ideas. Find or create places in your story where the character will break his or her own rules.

Another Maass exercise explores a character's desire and internal conflict.
1. Record what your character most wants.
2. Record the opposite of this want.
3. Freewrite: Show how your character could want both of these opposing things.

> ## "When you get into reality, nobody's black or white. There are shades of gray."
>
> MEL GIBSON, ACTOR

TRICKS OF THE TRADE

Lady and the Tramp. Beauty and the Beast. Butch Cassidy and the Sundance Kid. Any and every cop show. And, um, what's that vampire story with a love thing going on between a human and a vampire?

The Odd Couple.

The Odd Couple Construct shows up often. And for good reason. First, beneath this construct stands the literary tool of juxtaposition (or contrast). By setting opposites together, we immediately understand more about each. It's efficient characterization. Second, it sets up another "c" word: conflict. The Odd Couple supersizes conflict. Electricity snaps through differences.

By supplying a pair, this tool also immediately helps the writer avoid scene after scene of one character in his or her head. In other words, the Odd Couple Construct pulls the story into external action and dialogue.

BRAIN MATTER

Write It: Explain the Odd Couple Construct in your own words. Now think of a movie or novel that uses this construct. In your example, what conflict does the Odd Couple Construct use?

Chapter 8

POINT OF VIEW

Novelist Elizabeth Gaskell moved in the top literary circles of Victorian England. Charles Dickens? Her mentor and friend. Charlotte Brontë? Friend and ally.

Gaskell wrote novels that crackled with conflict and insight because of her deft use of point of view. For example, her 1855 novel, *North and South,* pits a wealthy factory owner, Mr. John Thornton, against the poverty-ridden worker and union leader, Mr. Nicholas Higgins. (Odd Couple Construct alert.)

When Higgins asks for employment, Thornton rudely dismisses him. Soon Thornton learns that Higgins had waited five hours to ask him. Shame assails him. This shame and his desire to be fair sends him through seedy alleys to the flat where the widower Higgins lives with his children and several orphans.

The smell. The poverty. The suffering. Thornton sees all. And as we walk along with Thornton, we see through this wealthy man's eyes.[1] Gaskell's choice lets us. Had she sent us along with Higgins, who likely simply walks past the squalor he calls home, we wouldn't have seen or felt it.

Point of view (POV) is our mighty tool. It moves our readers into experience and empathy.

How can we master POV in our writing? POV includes three main elements: viewpoint character, person and means of perception.

POV ELEMENT #1: VIEWPOINT CHARACTER

Viewpoint character: Who is telling the story?
Good news: Intuition cues us.
Bad news: Readers must care about this character.

Consider Sherlock Holmes and his narrating sidekick, Dr. Watson. Why is Watson the viewpoint character—the one who tells the story? Why not Holmes?

The answer is at least twofold. If brilliant Holmes was our viewpoint character,

Arthur Conan Doyle would be handcuffed. He wouldn't be able to unfold his mystery slowly. The suspense would plummet. Secondly, the brilliant but annoying Holmes as narrator would alienate us.

Those who know F. Scott Fitzgerald's novel, *The Great Gatsby,* may recall that Nick narrates Gatsby's life. Fitzgerald's choice to use a narrator other than Gatsby allows Gatsby to remain an enigma.

BRAIN MATTER

Write It: Explain the role of viewpoint character in your own words. What might we consider in deciding which of our characters ought to play this role?

POV ELEMENT #2: PERSON

Person: Do I use first person, second or third?
Good news: Often a comfort zone decision.
Bad news: Often a comfort zone decision.

Comfort zone may be the truest predictor of which person—first, second or third—we choose. Typically, we select either first person or third person.

Second person "you" shows up in experimental writing like flash fiction or nonfiction, and even in novels like the Nobel Prize–winning *Soul Mountain* by Gao Xingjian.

Some new writers might miss how intimate third person can be. In "Means of Perception," we'll explore how third person can be as intimate as first person.

BRAIN MATTER

Write It: Best advice tells us to go with our gut in settling on which person to use, but switching person in a freewrite may help us discover new insights. So, fast-draft a scene using a different person. What do you notice?

POV Element #3: Means Of Perception

Means of perception: Where is the movie camera positioned?
Good news: Offers us room to play.
Bad news: Moves in and out of vogue.

This final choice, means of perception, creates intimacy or distance. Means of perception shows us where the camera is stationed in relation to the characters. Where the camera is will guide us to which means of perception we use.

- Close (subjective)
- Omniscient
- Distant (objective)[2]

Means of Perception: Close

In close or subjective, the camera is only inside the viewpoint character's head. We look through this character's eyes and are privy to thoughts, emotional and physical sensations, actions and dialogue. Close may use either first or third person.

Close third person is having its day. Many recent bestsellers employ this means of perception. With psychology being part of our *zeitgeist,* this means of perception lets us sit in the front row of the character's thoughts. Its intimacy ensures our connection. It triggers our care connectors—or at least our curiosity.

This example of close third, also called single character subjective, demonstrates its intimacy:

Little Red pulled her cape. Its deep red wool seemed to glow in the dim forest light. Yeah, she was scared. But she was still going. Those silly old wolf stories. Those wouldn't keep her from Grandmother's house today.

Notice that we move seamlessly and without any signals into the character's thoughts.

In first person or close third, the camera rests behind the viewpoint character's eyes. The character can only see of herself what you can see of yourself: your hands, your eyeglass frames, the edge of your hair and so on.

Multiple character subjective is the same as single character subjective, but this means of perception allows us to move from character to character (one per scene, sometimes one per chapter). Rotating viewpoint characters can be catnip to reader and writer.

The young adult novel, *Wonder,* employs multiple character subjective. To signal a switch in viewpoint characters, author R. J. Palacio uses mechanical constructs like white space, a quote and the character's name. Interestingly enough, the movie also uses mechanical signals.[3]

Media critic Steven Johnson shows that since the 1980s, TV shows have grown in complexity—the number of threads or subplots and the number of characters.[4] We've become accustomed to and fond of seeing life from the eyes of multiple characters.

BRAIN MATTER

List It: If your character looks about him- or herself, what things does he or she see? Record.

Means of Perception: Omniscient

If we imagine a continuum, the omniscient means of perception falls between close and distant. Omniscient allows the narrator to reveal both inside and outside the character's head. Because the camera can swing from in the character to out, this means of perception may show everything from thoughts and emotional sensations to the character's appearance. It even may convey information beyond the viewpoint character's knowledge. Omniscient uses third person only.

Because many literature courses focus on modern literary works and not genre or commercial writing, some readers conclude that omniscient is the only means of perception. Ironically, though, while literary fiction still uses omniscient, writers like Renni Browne and Dave King consider this means of perception dated. They write, "You may think of omniscient narration as a nineteenth-century technique. And it's true that the omniscient point of view reached its most extreme form in nineteenth-century novels such as George Elliot's *Middlemarch*."[5]

Unlike multiple character subjective or close, omniscient may move in and out of multiple characters *within* a scene. While multiple character subjective does let us go into the heads of more than one character, we must wait for either a new scene or a new chapter. Limited omniscient, which on our continuum is one step toward close, allows the reader to go into only one character's head. How it differs from close, though, is that limited omniscient may go outside the character and beyond that character's knowledge.

BRAIN MATTER

Find It: Examine this example of the omniscient means of perception for places where the camera moves inside and outside of Little Red:

> The little girl, who wore a cherry red cloak, started her journey, determined to not be afraid. She was a stout lass with long blond curls that bounced at each step. That her journey took her through an ancient forest of sun-blocking cedars dating back to 1314 was only part of what made her journey dangerous. Although Little Red remained unaware, a shadow followed her a demure twenty-five feet behind. A man-eating wolf had chosen this day for the same journey.
>
> Little Red only knew that Grandmother needed her company and her food. Grandmother wasn't eating enough. Little Red smiled. Grandmother would love her blueberry muffins.

Means of Perception: Distant

In the distant or objective means of perception, the camera remains solely outside of the character's head. The reader must rely only on dialogue and actions, for readers aren't privy to the character's thoughts or emotional sensations. Like omniscient, only third person is used.

The 1920s to 40s showcased writers who used this external POV, such as Dashiell Hammett in his famous *The Maltese Falcon.* The detective genre perfected this means of perception. Recent bestsellers like Michael Chabon's *The Yiddish Policeman's Union,* also detective noir, use the distant means.

BRAIN MATTER

Find It: Examine this example of distant means for its use of external cues:

> Little Red's foot lowered onto the path. Layers of pine needles swallowed all sound. She stopped. While both hands clasped the picnic basket, her eyes moved side to side. Black-green shadows reached between the pines.
>
> She shuffled forward again. One hand left the basket handle to lift and

push against low limbs. The boughs bent forward and then as she passed, curled back to thunk her cape.

A fallen tree barred the path. The trunk reached almost to her hip. She scrambled up, but her leg swung over it without clearing. Her tights snagged bark. Little Red tried to vault over, but the front of the cape caught and halted her. She dropped the basket, pulled the cape edge from beneath her leg and finished shimmying over.

Leaves rustled.

"Hello!" Little Red turned around. "Hello? Is anyone there?"

Write It: In your own words, contrast two of our three means of perception. Which seems most familiar to you? Why?

COMMON ERROR: THE POV SLIP

A temptation surfaces in close third person: The POV Slip. This occurs when the POV is clearly anchored behind the eyes of one viewpoint character—and suddenly readers find themselves in the mind of a different character.

Hannah drummed her fingers. If she had only one more assignment to complete—then she could do late night ice cream with John. But. She had like five. And all due tomorrow. But there was John, waiting, with hope lifting his brows. He watched her, noting her fatigue. Hannah needed fun. That was obvious. She needed him.

Notice where the camera swings from behind Hannah's eyes to John's. Editors often consider this an error. Longtime fiction editor Andy Scheer calls this error "muddling the POV." In Ann Byle's *Christian Publishing 101,* Scheer says, "If novelists want readers to engage closely with the story, they need to be really careful with POV. This is one of the areas that novelists shoot themselves in the foot."[6] The longer your scene or story stays with a viewpoint character, says conventional wisdom, the more your reader bonds with that character.

POV LABELS

For some reason, POV attracts many different labels, varying by region or by which craft guru a writer adores.

Please note: some conflate limited omniscient and close third.

What may make this confusing is that the omniscient means of perception permits the camera to go behind multiple characters' eyes within one scene. Experimental writing like flash fiction allows this, too. But in typical single and multiple character subjective—in other words, close third—this is an error.

Notice how subtle this error can be in an example from creative writing student Linnae Conkel.[7] Her character Amani is the viewpoint character:

POV Slip Error

A scream decimated the air. Amani whirled around, locking eyes on the four girls. All of them stood stone still, fiery sticks clenched tightly in white-knuckled hands. Their eyes stared past Amani, wide and terrified like a horse spooked in a storm.

"Night creature," Suri whispered hoarsely.

Fear driving her body, the tall girl turned and fled. The others immediately followed suit, fire sticks and spark stones instantly forgotten. Amani watched them go, then, almost against her will, turned to see what the others had seen.

The viewpoint character seems to shift. The line "Fear driving her body" confuses the POV because it signals an internal sensation. We may wonder, *Oh, are we in Suri's head now?* Unclear pronoun reference adds confusion, too.

So, how can we revise this for a consistent POV? Conkel shows how simple changes can fix this common issue.

POV Slip Revised

A scream decimated the air. Amani whirled around, locking eyes on the four girls. All of them stood stone still, fiery sticks clenched tightly in white-knuckled hands. Their eyes stared past Amani, wide and terrified like a horse spooked in a storm.

"Night creature," Suri whispered hoarsely.

The tall girl's voice acted like a trigger and the four girls fled, fire sticks and spark stones instantly forgotten. Amani watched them go, then, almost against her will, turned to see what the others had seen.[8]

Conkel revised the POV Slip by replacing the internal sensation of the non-viewpoint character with an external cue, the sound of the voice. We, readers, now remain outside Suri's head and inside Amani's.

BRAIN MATTER

Write It: How does the three-prong POV (viewpoint, person and means of perception) differ from your previous learning? What's something in this chapter that you found confusing or thought-provoking?

Fastdraft It: Rewrite one of your scenes using a different means of perception.

Chapter 9

THE PLOT LENS

Plot is the cauldron of conflict, action and reaction within a story.

New York Times bestselling novelist Jacquelyn Mitchard suggests that a story runs like this: this happened and then this happened and then this happened, and so on.[1] In other words, we're talking cause and effect. Action and reaction. It is that basic.

Whether we're writing commercial or literary fiction, or trying to capture memoir, cause and effect powers our story forward. Something happens and that something triggers a response. And that response triggers yet another response.

The value we place on plot may, interestingly enough, depend on our writing process. Perhaps plotters—those who outline before drafting—see their way through plot more clearly than pantsers—those who write scenes where the idea is hot.

To imagine plot as something rigid, however, may hinder our writing. In fact, we have at least five lenses through which we can view and understand plot. As MFA instructor Bruce Holland Rogers explains, "Plot is any narrative structure that tends to create anxiety, anticipation or tension in the reader."[2]

LENS # 1: PLOT AS PYRAMID

Freytag's Pyramid stands as the most familiar image for plot. Literature classes still depend on this 1863 invention from the German novelist and playwright Gustav Freytag, whose five-act structure teaches us what is expected from plot.[3] (The well-known inciting incident wasn't part of Freytag's original categories.)

- Exposition: what the protagonist was like before conflict arrives
- Inciting incident: the event that sets change and conflict in motion
- Rising action: escalation of conflict from reactions meant to solve it
- Climax: the moment of final epiphany or most important action
- Falling action: the tension or conflict eases
- Dénouement: the final settling, resolution

BRAIN MATTER

Write It:

1. From Freytag's Pyramid, what three characteristics do you deduct about plot?
2. How can this construct help or hinder a writer?

LENS #2: PLOT AS THREE ACTS

In his *Writer's Digest* book *Plot Versus Character,* Jeff Gerke says that while some believe the Three-Act Structure is outdated or too formulaic, he sees this structure as classic—a worthy guide.[4]

Gerke notes that while Act I gives the needed context—yes, like Freytag's exposition—Act II contains the bulk of story action. Here, he says, conflict forces the internal problem, or knot within the protagonist, to become external.[5] "Your story," Gerke asserts, "is all about the middle."[6] The final act, of course, focuses on the end and resolution.

Plot points—that is, the story's pivots—are often the doorways to a new act, says author Dr. Joseph Bates.[7] For example, in *The Wizard of Oz,* the frightening tornado that lifts Dorothy from her normal life to a strange world serves as Plot Point One and twirls us into Act II.[8] The story's Plot Point Two happens when Dorothy meets the Wizard and must retrieve the witch's broom.

Some writers set plot points in predictable junctures, even down to a specific page. Fantasy writer K. M. Weiland asserts that the first plot point, known as both the inciting incident and the key incident, occurs 25 percent into the story. This event also functions as Act I's climax and signals the start of Act II.[9] Because Act II runs for 50 percent of the story, this section contains smaller plot points that Weiland and others name "pinch points."[10] The story's "centerpiece," the second significant plot point, marks the middle.[11] A third important plot point falls 75 percent into the story, heralding Act III.[12]

BRAIN MATTER

Apply It: Apply these percentages to your page count. Are the plot points occurring where these writes suggest?

TRUNCATED EXPOSITION

Twenty-first-century story craft has shortened Freytag's exposition stage. Compare the pace of a Charles Dickens novel like *A Tale of Two Cities* to a John Grisham.

Today we usually feather in background and avoid backstory clumps.

LENS #3: PLOT AS QUESTION

Beneath the cause and effect engine lurks questions—questions for which readers will travel page after page to answer.

- The Spine Question: main question running through entire (or almost entire) work

- Rib Questions: minor questions forming multiple subplots that heighten the suspense[13]

Every story has a spine question plus rib questions. The longer the work, the more rib questions. For example, think of a TV crime drama like *The Mentalist*. This drama had the spine question: Will Patrick Jane, our protagonist, find Red John, the killer who murdered his wife and children?

Each episode also offered several subplots that gave the story its rib questions. Someone was murdered; who did it? Other rib questions arise from the inevitable love interests or conflicts among the minor characters. A minor character wrestles addictions. Will he be OK?[14]

The Mentalist subverted its spine question in its second to the last season when Red John was killed. What emerged as the new spine question—and perhaps the real one all along—was this: will our co-protagonists finally admit their love?

(They did.)

BRAIN MATTER

Ponder It: Think about a favorite book or movie. What would you say is its spine question? What are two rib questions?

Write It: What is your story's spine question? Name two rib questions.

LENS #4: PLOT AS JOURNEY

Screenwriters know story craft. Along with understanding how to draft great dialogue, screenwriters often use the popular story model, the Hero's Journey, based on Joseph Campbell's work on myth and archetypes. This model offers us an effective lens through which to understand plot.

The Hero's Journey, depicted as a circle, instructs us in the timing or placement of key events and suggests archetypes, the fellow travelers, the protagonist may encounter.

If we imagine moving clockwise around a circle, the character receives and rejects the call to adventure. But when the clock hits 3, the character crosses "the threshold" and enters the journey—and Act II—with the help of a mentor. At 6 o'clock, the "central ordeal" occurs after the symbolic or actual entering a cave. Then the character rounds upward toward the "reward" and returns home.[15]

George Lucas famously applied the Hero's Journey in the *Star Wars* movies. Even the most recent sequel, *The Last Jedi,* by Rian Johnson, shows the Hero's Journey: Luke's call and dismissal of the call; Rey's entrance into the cave (like Luke's in *The Empire Strikes Back,* where he enters the cave to fight himself).

Characters are considered archetypes that offer a familiar cast from the mentor to the shapeshifter, i.e., the frenemy. We recognize the mentors, the wise guides, in the possibly clichéd insightful priest or the patiently loving mother.

But there are fresh ways to play archetypes. For example, ten-year-old Ashley Chandler, in *The Last Ship,* who instructs her dad, protagonist Admiral Tom Chandler, with her observation: "Mom wouldn't have wanted you to quit. You must go back." The smart admiral heeds his little girl.[16]

Lens #5: Plot as Change

Our characters travel through change, and for upmarket or literary fiction, this fact of being changed matters most. Unlike a plot-driven crime thriller where the familiar steps of solving the case power what happens next, short stories, literary novels or creative nonfiction writers may loosen their attention from elements of plot to focus on character change.

Literary critic and writer John Updike shows how to do this in his oft-anthologized short story, "Pigeon Feathers." We follow the bright but displaced fourteen-year-old David through a confrontation with his mortality and into an epiphany, or Adult Realization #352. The intricate beauty and construction of—literally—pigeon feathers settle his fear. And David is changed.[17]

Writer Ben Nyberg's *One Great Way to Write Short Stories* suggests three ingredients in successfully using character change as plot:

A. Show momentum of character's life
B. Show disruption
C. Show the person or character changed and in a new life momentum[18]

You already may have noted how Nyberg's categories relate to Freytag's Pyramid, our Plot Lens #1. The initial momentum echoes Freytag's exposition and the disruption, the inciting incident.

Writers who tend toward upmarket or literary fiction may be relieved to find that character change counts toward plot. In my rattling self-doubts about plotting my novel, MFA professor Bruce Holland Rogers assured me that my protagonist, Matthew Goodman, changes. And for my story, he announced, that was plot enough.

"Plot is the things characters do, feel, think or say that make a difference to what comes afterward."

Ansen Dibell,

Plot

BRAIN MATTER

Write It: We've examined five different lenses by which to understand plot: Plot as Pyramid, Plot as Three Acts, Plot as Question, Plot as Journey and Plot as Change. Explain one that struck you as interesting or applicable to your work. Which one enlarged the meaning of plot?

PLOT PLAY

New configurations of plots abound, which is part of creative play. Plot inventions can surprise and delight us.

- *Cloud Atlas* (novel): plot as an infinity loop
- *4 3 2 1* (novel): plot as four strands
- *Dunkirk* (film): plot as Act III only

What other books or films play with plot by using a nonlinear narrative?

Chapter 10
THE DIALOGUE KISS

Dialogue is our double agent that appears to be doing one thing while really doing another. Dialogue appears to be—and is, on one level—a conversation between characters. But dialogue must be hard at work doing several other tasks—its real tasks: furthering elements of story craft like characterization, plot, conflict.

"Dialogue is the illusion of speech in fiction. It may seem like a tape recording transcribed on paper, but it is . . . an artistic creation."

STEPHEN MINOT,
THREE GENRES

KEEP IT SHORT

The Keep It Short, but (Not Too) Sweet, the KISS approach, names good dialogue. Unless we have a character who loves the sound of his or her own voice, dialogue is short and grammatically incorrect. And often the better the characters know each other, the fewer words they say.

Take this scene from the long-running TV show *Numb3rs,* with its odd couple pairing of two brothers: Don Eppes, the older, who is athletic and popular; and Charlie Eppes, the younger, who is a misunderstood genius. Unfortunately, these differences had separated the brothers, but now in their thirties, Don and Charlie are trying to repair their relationship as they work together as FBI agents.

In one scene, Charlie realizes that Don had been serious about a woman now dead, and Charlie hadn't known about her or this significant relationship, which he regrets for Don's sake.

Listen to their spare exchange about Charlie's discovery:

Charlie: "I thought—"

Don: "I know."
Charlie: "Well?"
Don: "Yeah."[1]

Energy, movement and sparks abound. And in very few words. If we were writing this, we could easily supply nonverbal "showing" through action beats, which we'll discuss soon. Even without action beats, though, notice how effective short can be. When you and I speak, we don't say it all.

While we understand that dialogue and real speech have their differences, dialogue is similar to speech in that it also abuses grammar rules. You and I rarely speak in full, grammatically correct sentences. Characters don't either.

Tom eyed her. "Where to now?"

"There." Kate waved a hand.

"Not there!" Tom snorted. "Again?"

Dialogue also plays with punctuation. Listen to how these permutations send different messages and tones:

"Henry? Where are you?"

"Henry! Where are you!"

<hr>

ON-THE-NOSE DIALOGUE

On-the-nose dialogue sounds like we're holding a gun to our characters and making them say what we want.

Example: "Stacy, I'm acting out in class because when I was twelve my classmate died of leukemia. Since I'm only eighteen now, I haven't yet processed my grief."

Enough said. Critique partners or beta readers help detect this dialogue misstep.

BRAIN MATTER

Write It: Put into your own words what you're noticing about writing dialogue.

Not Too Sweet

Dialogue ain't real speech. It doesn't meander like real speech. It doesn't exchange pleasantries.

Dialogue must have some conflict or it's stale. In *Stein on Writing,* veteran editor Sol Stein insists on a vital and energizing ingredient in dialogue: the competing script.[2]

So, what is a competing script?

On a basic level, it happens when characters are at odds. (Yes, recall the Odd Couple Construct.) To create a competing script, we assign different desires, purposes or motives to our characters, which, of course, surface when they speak. Competing scripts lift dialogue and ignite conflict.

Compare the energy between these two examples of dialogue.

Without competing scripts:

"Hi, how are you, Sara?"

"I'm great. And you?"

With competing scripts:

"Hi." Nan studied Sara. "How are you?"

Sara looked away. "Fine. Real fine."

Setting aside how helpful the action beats are, how would you explain the competing scripts between Sara and Nan? What does it do to their brief exchange?

BRAIN MATTER

Find It: Creative writing student Caleb Dierolf penned this scene as he interviewed Thatch, his character, whom Caleb was getting to know. After you read this exchange, explain how a competing script surfaces between Thatch and narrator. How would you name it?

I sit across from the rugged, older man at the corner table in the back of the tavern.

"You're late," he grumbles into his mug of ale.

"Um, yeah, sorry about that. I came as quickly as I could."

Thatch puts his mug back down on the table. "Oh, well. You said you wanted to ask me a few questions?"

"Yes, actually. Is that alright with you?"

"Depends on the questions."

"Ah—"

"Well, you start askin', and I'll answer questions I want to answer." He takes another swig.

"Right. Mr. Thatch, what irritates you the most?"

"Small talk."

"Alrighty then . . . perhaps a meatier question. Would you mind telling me about your childhood? What were your parents like?"

"Dunno. Never met 'em." Another drink.

"I see . . . well, how were you raised then?"

Thatch's dark green eyes blink at me in irritation as he crosses his arms. "Next question."[3]

Write It: Fast-draft a dialogue exchange using competing scripts between two roommates, one of which is a little careless and is approaching the other to borrow an expensive car.

DIALOGUE TAGS & ACTION BEATS

Dialogue tags and action beats do the important work of cueing who is speaking. We're clear now that, like the fashion world, writing follows trends that come and go. In much twenty-first-century writing, the action beat—a term taken from the world of scriptwriting—has usurped the dialogue tag and for good reason. But first, let's define each.

Dialogue tags, underlined below, cue speakers and the verbal delivery—who is saying it and how it's said.

"Hi, Karen," <u>he said.</u>

"Hi, Karen," <u>he whispered.</u>

<u>Karen yelled,</u> "Goodbye!"

Notice that dialogue tags use commas to join the sentence. These tags don't stand alone. They aren't complete sentences.

Action beats cue speakers by stating a nonverbal action.

"Hi, Karen." Bob fumbled with his collar.

Karen turned away. "Goodbye, Bob."

Action beats have muscled into popular writing, often replacing dialogue tags. Why? They're efficient. They're strong speaker identification and showing. Unlike dialogue tags, action beats stand apart as separate sentences.

BRAIN MATTER

Punctuate It: Punctuate these action beats and dialogue tags.

1.   He sneezed Gosh! Excuse me
2.   You're excused. You just look so funny when you sneeze I said
3.   Well, rub it in he said, smiling

DIVERSE VOICES

Joe Harman, the Australian cattleman in *A Town Like Alice,* habitually concedes, "You're too right" or "It's a fair cow."[4] *Merriam-Webster* defines the latter slang for me: "exceedingly troublesome."[5] Who knew? Australians knew.

Our speech patterns are riddled with clues about our geographical region, personality, habits, generation, occupation and so on. What don't we reveal when we speak?

Think of word choice alone.

- Age or generation: Do you say "couch" or "davenport," "chill" or "cool"?
- Geographical region: Do you say "soda" or "pop," "runners" or "tennis shoes"?

As we listen, we'll hear the word our character uses repeatedly as she launches into an angry tirade. Or how another character interrupts and overspeaks others.

If a little smile is lifting your lips, you're right. This is fun.

BRAIN MATTER

Consider It: Study a piece of nonfiction or fiction that uses multiple viewpoint characters (*Wonder* or Hugh Cook's *Heron River* are excellent fiction samples). How do these writers create different voices? Compare two characters. Cite examples of how the difference in voice is created (e.g., sentence length).

Write It: Create different voices in your dialogue by brainstorming these prompts for two characters:

- Name
- Level of diction
- Pet buzzwords
- Favorite swear words
- Preferred metaphors
- Length of sentences or turn-taking

Chapter 11
SETTING

The scene opens. A fast-moving train winds up a mountain pass. Steep ridges drop into sheer gorges. The camera pans into an opened baggage car where double agent Sydney Bristow kicks her assailant. Hard. Physics propels Sydney backwards—and out the door. She grabs baggage straps and dangles. Wind powers her hair; she flails. Below her, train wheels screech and the gorge gapes.

Then *Alias* feature, "The Anatomy of a Scene: Train Fight" cuts to reality. Now we see actress Jennifer Garner dangling above—not a mountain gorge—but a blue screen and yellow tennis balls.

Tension deflates like a punctured balloon.

Visual effects supervisor Kevin Blank says that famed director J. J. Abrams asked for a moving train and for the team of experts to "generate an environment that was believable."[1]

Without it, beloved star Ms. Garner looks . . . well . . . silly. Why? The lack of setting sinks verisimilitude. A lack of setting wakes viewers or readers from imagination's dream.

> "Prose is architecture, not interior decoration."
> Ernest Hemingway

Setting as Verisimilitude

Our use of setting isn't the frosting on the cake; it is the cake. Without setting, our story doesn't work. Our old friends that we met in Chapter 5—specifics and the senses—help us avoid the blue screen effect.

Specifics details and the senses build the needed quality of verisimilitude. Verisimilitude is the feel of reality an author creates that convinces us that this place and this story is real. Verisimilitude is key to world building.

In Chapter 6, we then examined the description continuum from maximalists like Tom Clancy, who wrote with infamous detail (think submarine engines), to minimalists like Maeve Binchy (*Tara Road*), who dribbles description.

To gauge the right amount of description requires holding in tension our preferences with our reader's ability to see and experience the scene.

Reader feedback can serve us well here. Is the reader entering into our story? Does the story feel real and alive? If not, with a lack of verisimilitude, we may be giving our readers the blue screen effect. We don't know until we ask. Being workshopped or critiqued can guide us.

When I was revising my novel manuscript, *The Surface of Water,* I encountered a blue screen effect that was obvious enough for me to detect.

The story unfolds in Chicago, a city I don't know well. This scene takes place in a library downtown—a library that I've never visited:

> Trish scanned the pedestrians behind her before climbing the expansive steps to the Chicago Public Library. She pushed through glass doors and inhaled the familiar smell of books and cleaner. She found an unused flat screen, and sliding into a hard black seat, wrestled her backpack for the legal pad.

I found this scene lacking in "particularity—detail that individualizes," as Stein calls specifics.[2] So, because I couldn't visit Chicago, I did the next best thing. I googled Chicago. I learned street names and locations and studied pictures. I found the Harold Washington Library and went on its virtual tour.

Armed with specific details, I revised the scene. Notice how the use of specifics improves this scene's verisimilitude:

> Trish pushed like a salmon as she wove through currents of Saturday shoppers on State Street. The red granite walls of the Harold Washington Library loomed closer, its five-story windows reflecting cloud and sky. *Investigation* was the word for the day. Trish scanned the pedestrians behind her before entering through the tall glass door. The familiar smell of books and lemon cleaner welcomed her.
>
> The escalator clicked as it deposited her on the third floor where beneath her feet spread gray and white geometrical patterns. She hurried to the room's south side where people hunched near monitors.

This revised section—revised through light research—eliminates the blue screen effect through our old friends, specifics and the senses.

BRAIN MATTER

Write It:

1. Without doing any research, write a paragraph describing the trail that winds through the Grove of the Patriarchs in Mt. Rainier National Park, Washington.
2. Now google Mt. Rainier National Park and study descriptions and pictures of the Grove of the Patriarchs.
3. Revise your first paragraph. Add in your newly learned specifics.
4. Explain what you notice. What did you and your writing gain by simple research?

SETTING AS SOUL REVEAL

Reveal the hidden. Show, don't tell. These mottos can haunt us as we write. How do we accomplish our story goals without "telling"? How do we move our readers or cue them?

One answer: let setting act as psychological revelation.

Setting can be trusted to do double duty. We know that setting literally grounds the story. Setting also can reveal the soul of a character.

Like our characters, you and I view every object, everything, through our subjective experience. Someone who was badly scratched by a Siamese cat will likely cock a skeptical eye when a friend's Siamese approaches. If you're a movie lover, though, you may think, "Oh! *Lady and the Tramp.*"

Setting can help reveal our characters' subjective lens—in other words, their soul.

For example, this description of setting by Cornerstone University student Abby Wakeman delivers clues about her fictional character who is a lonely runaway:

All that he had as a reference point was a tall, leafless oak tree. The tree's bark was stripped down, barely being held together by the thinnest fragments of oak.[3]

Wakeman tutors us about her viewpoint character. That he is like the striped tree—and that he isn't doing well. The setting reveals his soul.

In Disney's first full-color, full-length animation, *Snow White* (1938), a scene reveals the protagonist's soul or state of being. To flee danger, Ms. White races through dark woods. The Disney animators drew trees with faces whose limbs ended in human hands—witchey hands. Personification aside, Snow White's fright—her inner turmoil—transformed the woods into threatening creatures. Through the setting we understand Snow White; we get her soul—her fear.[4]

This soul reveal benefits key scenes—dramatic scenes—where we want to heighten a reader's connection.

How do we do this? Build a description of the physical setting, what the character sees, through the character's emotional lens. Metaphors, similes and other such tools will do the work.

The poignant short story, "A Simple Matter of Hunger" by Sharon Oard Warner, reveals the main character's perspective when she and the AIDS baby she's fostering linger in a doctor's waiting room. Eleanor likens the apple pin, a character prop, worn by one receptionist to be "as red as Snow White's apple."[5] A poisoned apple? We then understand the tension Eleanor feels in this office where help ultimately will fail.

BRAIN MATTER

Write It: Let a viewpoint character's subjective experience color his or her world. Imagine a maple tree in autumn with flaming red leaves.

1. Describe a red leaf from the viewpoint of someone who is newly engaged and happy.
2. Describe a red leaf from the viewpoint of a vampire.

Now explain what you notice about deepening setting by revealing the character's soul.

Chapter 12

SCENES: STORY BRICKS

Imagine a brick wall or a house where careful hands have put into place brick after brick. If we gather enough of these small blocks, a sizeable object arises. Like our imagined wall or house, essays and books are built with small units, too: the scene.

The contents of any scene are our now-familiar "Show, don't tell" tools: action, description, dialogue, etc. In other words, story craft will be at work. A scene must have action. Characters are moving, thinking, speaking "over a set period of 'real' time."[1]

A scene requires something else: change. In fact, it may be helpful to compare a scene to a short story. A mini-inciting incident shifts normal life, tension increases—and the character arrives at a new state of being.

Janet Burroway in her premier text explains, "Like a story, on its own small scale, a scene has a turning point or mini-crisis that propels the story forward toward its conclusion."[2] Narrative nonfiction benefits from this construction, too.

CHANGE AS IMPETUS

"And how was your day?" Dave stood near the stove as I stirred the refried beans and hamburger.

"Oh . . ." I had spent the day revising my novel, working hard to order my scenes better. "It's heavy lifting right now. My brain seized up."

Dave eased onto the black stool. My counselor hubby grew intent. "Seized? You need a guiding structure."

"I've got a guiding structure." I stirred. "I had to pull my minor plot out of Act I. But now I've got a big clump of it in Act II. I have to feather it in better."

"Well, here it becomes three-dimensional."

I stopped stirring.

"This can guide your interspersing." Dave's hands made a globe. "Goodman moves closer, Trish moves farther." His left hand moved toward his right hand, but the latter retreated, keeping his hands the same distance apart as if they still held the globe.

Energy zipped through me. I understood. Within each scene, there could be this movement.

I fastened on a new metaphor. "Or like a teeter-totter? One character goes down and the other goes up?"

"Exactly. Weave this into your subplot like a dance step. Like a DNA helix."

New York Times bestselling novelist Julie Cantrell offers a similar idea in scene pacing. She even chalks her good sales to this strategy: one scene the character is up and goes down, the next the character is down and goes up.[3]

Movement and tension create impetus, and impetus crackles with energy.

Exactly what we want, precisely what we need.

Narrative Summary

Most rules have shortcomings, so we can understand that even "Show, don't tell" has its limits. We must tell at times, and telling can hasten the pace. Narrative summary is an effective form of telling because it helps us bypass dull details or avoid repeating character actions.

Narrative summary reads like this:

- After the call, Sam returned to work. (Omits phone conversation.)
- Karen hurried through the paperwork. (Skips dull step-by-step detail.)
- Dennis completed the investigation. (Replaces an oft-repeated character task with narrative summary.)
- Donna explained the accident. (Avoids repeating a previous scene.)

Narrative summary accelerates the pace and helps us to skip the redundant.

While revising my sequel, *The Redemption of Pastor Goodman,* I found this dull scene:

The small, family-owned hotel had offered her a quiet place for sleep. The abundant flower pots and good mattress had assured her its quality.

"Are you checking out the university?" the young clerk had asked.

"No. Just stopping by. Is that the big draw?"

"Oh, yeah, yeah, yeah. That's why people come."

"Nice."

"We're a great town. We're always in the top of highest satisfaction for hometown surveys for Iowa. We've got the lowest crime rate of any other Iowa city. Stuff like that. You should take a look around."

See what I mean? Dull. Did this need to be a full-fledged scene with dialogue that unfolds in story time? No. I replaced this unneeded yawn with a fast-paced line of narrative summary:

> The small family-owned hotel gave Trish two gifts, the knowledge that Glenwood was a university town and sleep.

BRAIN MATTER

Revise It: Shrink this unneeded scene into narrative summary:

> John swung down from the combine. He stretched the long muscle that tethered rib to spine, spine to hip, and anchored all to the pelvis. He groaned as he stretched his legs. His knees complained of the long jarring hours in the combine.
>
> His father walked toward him, listing to the right. Knees and backs were casualties of farming, and his dad hadn't escaped. Neither would he.
>
> So far his dad had resisted a knee replacement—despite his mom's frequent arguments.
>
> "Been a good day, son." The older Newbury stopped near John. Summer had added new lines around his father's eyes.
>
> "Yeah." John swung an arm around his father's shoulders and felt them stiffen. Neither of his parents had hugged him much in his boyhood. On occasions, his father would pat his shoulder, but it had been John who had initiated the hugging, the stepping too near another and embracing him whole. His father still stiffened, but his face would soften and change.
>
> Char had taught him how to hug his father.

BRAIN MATTER

Write It: Describe in your own words what you learned or were reminded of in our discussion about scenes.

SECTION IV

Craft Pizzazz

Chapter 13

THE INTENSIFIERS

How do we build intensity, drama, pace as we hurtle toward the plot climax or character epiphany?

1. Description
2. Sentence construction and length
3. Poetic tools

Surprised? Let's examine how these intensifiers up drama.

INTENSIFIER#1: DESCRIPTION

We're clear now that description—built from specifics and the senses—creates our world, the feel of reality, the verisimilitude. We know that, in characterization, description fleshes out the people we've imagined. Description can even add a psychological layer to setting.

But description has another role. It acts as a pointing arrow. It emphasizes. It says to our readers, "Pay attention."

We know this craft fact when it comes to major and minor characters; we know to spend less time describing minor ones. A waiter, when only a minor character, may get only "the short, dark-haired waiter." If we spend more space describing this waiter and even name him, our reader might expect to see this character again.

The zany Tim Allen movie *Galaxy Quest* teaches us this lesson with a laugh. This science fiction parody of *Star Trek* introduces a group of once-famous TV actors who find themselves in an alien culture. The aliens mistake the TV show *Galaxy Quest* for "cultural history," and worse, have taken the actors aboard their spacecraft, expecting them to know how to run a starship. One scene illustrates my point about minor characters. A shuttle carries the main characters to a planet where they must search for beryllium spheres. Among them is Dr. Lazarus (Alan Rickman) and Commander Taggart (Tim Allen). Also on board is a minor character, Guy, played by comedian Sam Rockwell.

As they approach the planet, Guy's face twists. He whines, "I change my mind. I want to go back."

Dr. Lazarus snaps, "All that fuss you've made at getting left behind!"

"Yeah," says Guy, "but that's when I thought I was the crew member that stays on the ship and gets killed, but now I'm thinking I'm the guy who gets killed by some monster five minutes after we land on the planet and—"

Commander Taggart barks, "You're not going to die on the planet, Guy!"

"I'm not? What's my last name?"

"Ummm," the commander stalls. "I don't know."

"Nobody knows! Do you know why? Because my character's not important enough for a last name because I'm going to die—"[1]

This metafictional conversation hints at this craft fact: key characters, events and moments get more ink. Thus we understand description's additional role. Description functions as a pointing arrow. Description signals importance.

Let's continue to explore how we can use description with the help of famous suspense director Alfred Hitchcock. To up intensity or signal significance, Hitchcock favored extreme close-ups. The famous shower scene? His camera zooms in; the showerhead fills the screen. The glass of bedtime milk carried upstairs by the husband who might just be poisoning his wife? The camera tightens onto the glass. Let's coin the famous director's signal the "Hitchcockian close-up."

You want to heighten a scene's intensity or signal an object's importance? Create a close-up for your reader through vivid description. Focus your reader's eye on the object through the pointing arrow of description, a verbal close-up.

Hitchcockian close-ups—adding more description—serve moments of epiphany, too. In the following excerpt, John, a widowed farmer, suspects his brother Nate is taking things from the homestead where John lives:

John closed the front door and locked it. Something propelled him forward. He moved slowly through the house, opening closets, more drawers. He climbed the stairs and brushed through the bedrooms.

What could Nate want? Maybe Jimmy was acting alone. He saw them again exchange the high five. No. Something was up with Nate. But what?

He descended the stairs and turned toward the living room. The small oak desk stood against the west wall where a decade ago the family farm was run. He approached it.

Its middle drawer, long and narrow, jutted outwards slightly. Everything in the room disappeared except for that right edge where a slice of unstained wood pushed past the desk lip. He clutched its handle and pulled.

The last paragraph tightens the camera onto the oak desk and its jutting drawer. This shows how a Hitchcockian close-up emphasizes an object and places a pointing arrow of significance above it. We readers feel it and focus.

BRAIN MATTER

Consider It: Study a Hitchcockian close-up in action on YouTube. Search "Suspicion Milk Scene" for one of the most famous close-ups in Hitchcock's career, from the movie *Suspicion* (1941). Is the milk a loving gesture from a loving husband—or is this man a murderer carrying a glass of poisoned milk?

Write It: Intensify through description:
1. Pick a nearby object.
2. List its specific details.
3. Now shape a Hitchcockian close-up by transforming the list into a paragraph.

Revise It: Check a dramatic scene in your writing for its use of description and intensify by adding specific detail.

INTENSIFIER #2: SENTENCES

Sentence construction and length can quicken or slow our pace and up intensity. In other words, sentences can act as a brake or an accelerator pedal.

Sentence Construction

Our use of grammar and punctuation affects pace. Anytime we don't start with the subject, we slow our pace. So, introductory phrases or clauses suspend the reader before the main subject and verb appear, which slows the reading pace. The following examples demonstrate:

Introductory Phrase or Clause
- After Sara walked to the window, she spoke.
- Because he liked her, Curt bought her flowers.

On the other hand, putting our subject first ups our pace:

Subject First or S-V-O Construction
- Sara faced the window.
- Curt bought the girl he liked flowers.

BRAKES	ACCELERATORS
Introductory phrases or clauses	Subject-verb-object sentences
Interrupters (nonrestrictive clauses)	Run-on sentences and fragments
Same-length sentences	Very long or short sentences
Passive voice, passive verbs	Active voice, active verbs
Long paragraphs	Short paragraphs

Sentence Length

Can our reader move through our sentences with ease? We find one answer in our sentence lengths. How many words we pack into a sentence plus the number of syllables in those words impact what publishers call "readability."

In critical scenes, shortening or lengthening sentences works magic. But what exactly is a long sentence? Or, for that matter, a short one? The following chart on page 84 answers the question of how word count affects readability.[2]

First, skim the chart and then observe how Steven James uses short sentences in this scene below from *Placebo* where the protagonist realizes he's being followed:

Glenn could hardly believe it.

The two people angling toward him were the ones who'd been in the chamber last night.

Don't let them see you!

He slipped into his car and tilted the rearview mirror. Watched them climb into a sedan not fifty feet away.

No indication they'd noticed him.

Good.[3]

SENTENCE LENGTH	READABILITY
8 words or less	Very easy
11 words	Easy
17 words	Standard
21 words	Fairly difficult
25 words	Difficult
29 words	Very difficult

BRAIN MATTER

Consider It: Record the number of words in each sentence in the *Placebo* excerpt. Compare to the readability chart. What sentence construction tools does James use?

Film student Elizabeth Okma revised her prison fight scene with short in mind:

> Instinct takes over. My racing heart slows. He grins before plunging the taser again towards me. I grip his wrist, twisting his arm. His fingers release the taser. It hits the ground with a flat thud as our eyes lock. I throw my elbow into his face. His head jerks. I release his arm and drive my foot into his chest. He staggers back. His feet squeak against the concrete.[4]

Okma's short sentences hasten the pace—needed in an action scene.

Strangely enough, a very long sentence speeds us through content, too. Marilynne Robinson starts with a 42-word sentence in her Pulitzer-Prize winning *Gilead.* Her opening lines capture a conversation between an older man late to fatherhood and his child:

> I told you last night that I might be gone sometime, and you said, Where, and I said, To be with the Good Lord, and you said, Why, and I said, Because I'm old, and you said, I don't think you're old.[5]

This tender quote is a fast read, made faster by Robinson's omission of quotation marks.

Another famous writer, Frederick Buechner, opens his memoir, *Telling Secrets,* with an even longer sentence: eighty words. What craft decisions might Robinson and Buechner have made in making their first sentences long?

BRAIN MATTER

Write It: Allowing for a "crappy first draft," move through these prompts to play with the wonderful intensifier of sentence construction and length:

1. List it: Details from a street corner and road with sidewalk activity.
2. List it: Car careens onto the sidewalk, hits store window.
3. Fast-draft: Use short sentences.
4. Rewrite into long sentences.

Apply It: Check a dramatic scene in your writing for the use of sentence length. Choose two mid-scene paragraphs and count words per sentence. What do you notice? Now play with length. Try short. Try long. What seems to work best?

WRITING LEVEL

If you're interested in calculating your writing level, one of these following tools can help: the Flesch-Kincaid Index, the Gunny-FOG Index or the SMOG Index. If you're interested in an excellent discussion of word economy, find a copy of *On Writing Well* by William Zinsser—whose multi-decade bestseller is considered excellent.

INTENSIFIER #3: POETIC TOOLS

Say the word "poetic" and some writers start to sweat. No worries. We're not talking about the difficult poetic moves of meter or feet, but rather two familiar tools that can serve our prose. Repetition and figurative language are likely old friends, although we may not have realized what good friends they are.

- Repetition creates rhythm or lyrical sound, emphasis and intensity.
- Figurative language heightens emphasis and deepens meaning.

Repetition

Dr. Martin Luther King Jr. had jumped off-script by the time he began repeating, "I have a dream."[6]

We hear in his repetition a cadence, a beat. His repetition imprints the dream on our souls. When we repeat words or word phrases, we usher in the power of music: beats, rhythms, stresses. The repetition makes it memorable.

We increase intensity with the simple and effective use of repetition. Take this example of children at play from Gary D. Schmidt's Newbery Honor winner, *Lizzie Bright and the Buckminster Boy*:

> Two of them grabbed Turner's hands. "Fly with us!" cried one. And they pulled him up and suddenly he was flapping his arms and running down the beach, and Lizzie was flapping hers and running alongside them, together in the midst of the swarm, and calling and calling and running and running.[7]

In this excerpt, we hear the cadence that repetition brings. The cadence adds sound and intensifies the moment.

Victorian novelist Elizabeth Gaskell uses subtle repetition in *North and South* to intensify character Margaret Hale's mental anguish over her brother's life: "Then she began to recall, to combine, to wonder."[8] The simple repetition of "to" creates a rhythm and intensity. Gaskell also plays with asyndeton when she omits the serial "and"—further tightening intensity.

Anaphora is a type of repetition that repeats the same words or phrases at the start of neighboring sentences. In the heart-sizzling essay by Brian Doyle, "Joyas Voladoras," the words "a hummingbird's heart" is repeated at the start of several sentences.[9] He also repeats, "Consider the hummingbird," an effective intensifier.

Repetition builds momentum and power. It fastens the moment in our memory. It underscores meaning. And, well, it's beautiful. (It's also easy.) Repetition serves us writers well in moments of epiphany or in conclusions.

Figurative Language

That metaphors, similes, personification and the like are old friends—that we, in fact, often march them out with great ease and perhaps little thought—in no way minimizes their power. Figurative language is the language of our gut. A well-crafted metaphor ignites deep meaning within our core.

Power intensifies when figurative language is used:

Weak: Butterflies emerge with crumpled wings.
Stronger: "The wings, the butterfly's glory, start all crumpled, like a wad of paper covered in mistakes."[10]

Writer Savanna DeWolf's simile surprises. It's fresh and powerful.

Why does figurative language (i.e., images) empower writing? "Images activate the five senses," says Hope College professor and memoirist Heather Sellers.[11]

This same poetic tool often appears in nonfiction. In "Under the Influence," the marvelous essayist Scott Russell Sanders uses an image to convey his perception of his dad—and captures the emotional meaning for a kid whose father is a mean alcoholic:

All evening, until our bedtimes, we tiptoe past him, as past a snoring dragon. Then we curl in our fearful sheets, listening.[12]

A father seen as a dragon? In our gut we understand. This father radiates danger.

TRICKS OF THE TRADE

A sophisticated maneuver that uses metaphors is the objective correlative. An objective correlative is a math term that in literary circles signals an extended metaphor. This tool charges our writing.

For example, think of Psalm 23, which carries an objective correlative. Through the chapter, comparisons are made between God and a protective shepherd and how we are sheep. The psalmist relies on image after image—an image cluster—related to all things "sheep."

The Ellen Douglas novel *Can't Quit You, Baby* cues us about her protagonist with an objective correlative that is pulled through the entire novel. Again and again, Cornelia and her refusal to acknowledge the less-than-perfect aspects of life is likened to a water-skier.[13] This character? She stays on the surface. This woman doesn't go deep.

Another famous southern writer mentioned earlier, Eudora Welty, deftly braids multiple objective correlatives through "Death of the Traveling Salesman" to disclose the soul of her character, R.J. Bowman.

In the following example, Welty narrows her use of figurative language to intensify Bowman's epiphany—that how he's chosen to live has kept him apart and isolated. Welty slides from the physical heart to the emotional heart with the objective correlative of water:

> . . . he wanted to leap up, to say to her . . . how lonely I am. My heart . . . should be full, he would rush on to tell her, thinking of his heart now as a deep lake, it should be holding love like other hearts. It should be flooded with love.[14]

Notice that Welty equates Bowman's heart with a lake and then carries it forward. The story continues developing this objective correlation.

As mentioned in Chapter 4, while revising my novel manuscript, *The Surface of Water,* I realized that I needed to heighten my protagonist's epiphany. So I recorded Welty's passage to see how she did it. I studied her craft moves. Then I revisited my scene and wrote this image-laden paragraph, using my own objective correlative:

> Goodman surveyed his office, the half-closed adjoining door. He needed to close it against her. But the door might as well have been light years away. He could not rise. His body pressed limply against his chair. He was a man in space, dark, without close light, shards of distant stars frozen and beyond reach, beyond warmth. He was that man floating beyond where gravity could control. He was too loose.[15]

This new objective correlative with its outer space images strengthened Goodman's epiphany and the scene's intensity. I thanked Welty and clicked "save."

BRAIN MATTER

Review It: Translate the intensifiers into your words: description, sentence construction and length and poetic tools. Is there one you already use? Which one might be fun to experiment with?

Consider It: Scour this excerpt from Frank Peretti's *Prophet,* where the protagonist, Carl, finds himself at a rock concert. Pinpoint where the intensifiers are used:

> Then came the sound. The sound. The crowd gave itself to the sound. It pounded through their chests, grabbed them by their guts, clutched their hearts, cut into their minds. It led, they followed; it soared, they flew; it crashed, they cried; it thundered, they roared; it leaped, they danced.

It took them it took them it grabbed them and took them it ripped them and it tore and it pounded and took them the drums and the lights and the cry of the strings and the smoke and the sweat and the volley of screams took them on. And on. And on. And on.[16]

Apply It:

1. List Three: What are recurring images in your story—or possible images?
2. Revisit one of your dramatic scenes. Where can you roll the scene forward with repetition or introduce figurative language?

Chapter 14

WHITE SPACE

White space, the places on a page without lettering or graphics, offers our stories a punch of acceleration—and, ironically enough, a place to handle deep emotion. You'll notice white space in margins, indentations and so on.

New York Times bestselling author Lorilee Craker had published for twenty years when editors began requesting something new: lots of white space, please.

Craker obeyed. "Everyone finds white space appealing and inviting, as opposed to tons of text, which intimidates the reader," she says. "When editors pick the manuscript off the slush pile, you want to invite them, not dissuade them."[1]

Point taken.

White space offers us writers several virtues: increased reader comprehension and scene emphasis, and in pain-filled topics, even sacred space.

This trend began over a decade ago when word count plunged downward. For example, today many nonfiction editors want manuscripts that hover at 50,000-75,000 words. Young adult fiction comes in at 40,000 words. Even much adult fiction has shrunk from an average of 100,000 words to 90,000.

If we study Flannery O'Connor's 1952 novel *Wise Blood,* we see that most of its pages offer long sentences and paragraphs. The lack of white space gives the page a gray tone. Some pages even contain the unimaginable: one long unbroken paragraph. O'Connor's enviable work may be showing its age. In fact, by looking at a book's use of white space, we may be able to guess its era.

According to graphic designer Vitaly Friedman's article "White Space and Simplicity: An Overview," Web design has driven the crusade for increased white space. This "less is more" trend grew out of psychological experiments on using white space for reading comprehension and emphasis.[2] A study in *The Journal of Experimental Psychology* shows that "white space around the highlighted items tends to increase their prominence."[3] Another study says that reading comprehension lifts 20 percent when white space is used.[4]

Interesting for us writers.

White space also gives readers a subjective sense that designers call "breathing." Design guru Mark Boulton explains this sense: "White space creates breathing room and balance."[5]

Think about how we might use this tool. An emotionally raw story may be easier to read if we inflate its white spaces.

Newbery-winner *The One and Only Ivan* by Katherine Applegate is a middle grade novel told from viewpoint character Ivan, a silverback ape.[6] Young readers must navigate hard topics like a depressed ape, mistreatment of animals and an elephant's death. Applegate's use of immense white space moves her readers through the sad parts, a helpful technique that verse writers like Karen Hesse employ.

Hesse's Newbery-winning *Out of the Dust*—a novel told in verse—is an unflinchingly grim story that tells young Billie Jo's experience of life in the Dust Bowl and of a fire that kills her mother and destroys Billie Jo's piano-playing hands. Sometimes only two or three words appear on a line. For example, Hesse narrates the fire scene like this:

I got
burned
bad.[7]

This immense white space concentrates these words, creating a words-as-paragraph effect that lets the reader experience horror while simultaneously easing the horror.

White space also serves painful nonfiction topics. When beloved Calvin and Yale professor Dr. Nicholas Wolterstorff lost his son in a mountain climbing accident, he began a grief journal. Later his journal was published as the beautiful *Lament for a Son*.

Some pages in this poignant work carry mostly white space while holding only one short gut-wrenching paragraph. The surrounding empty space allows a sense of quietness—perhaps even a sacred silence. It's as if Wolterstorff built a high cathedral ceiling above his words where the reader can sit in silence and feel before more words prod him or her forward.

Why did this grieving father and scholar use wide berths of space? Because as Wolterstorff wisely observes about white space: "In the face of death, we must not chatter."[8]

Like any other good technique, use of white space can be overdone. At times while grading, I coax my student writers to couple their sentences into fuller paragraphs.

One-sentence paragraph after one-sentence paragraph can have a staccato effect. Soon this overuse of white space loses its power.

But if the scene is dramatic or the line of thought is strategic, leave the white space. Trust it.

BRAIN MATTER

Consider It: Thumb through your pages. How long are your paragraphs? How short? Describe your use of white space. Where might you use it for effect?

Chapter 15

TIME TRAVEL

Whether we write experimental fiction or traditional nonfiction, using flashback can carry readers to a pivotal moment that affects a story's present. Although a common craft move, creating a smooth entrance into and exit out of a flashback can challenge us. How can we move our reader back and forth smoothly through time?

Let's first remind ourselves what must change grammatically when we time travel into the past. For one or two sentences, we'll need to add "had" to our verbs. In other words, we shift into the past perfect tense. This construction, "had + verb," creates a one- or two-sentence time machine.

For example, in this scene's present time, Pastor Matthew Goodman enters his father's study, a study that is preserved as a shrine to the famous radio evangelist. Notice where adding "had" signals entrance into the flashback:

> Goodman approached the chair, clasped its wooden armrest and sat. The chair creaked as if dismayed to serve another Goodman. A worn black King James Bible lay to his left. Past the birdcage, album covers of radio programs and photos spotted the wall. Father would have been furious: nail holes in the oak? He arched his fingers over the typewriter keys as he glanced to the doorway.
>
> Goodman had arrived at a similar doorway outside Father's study, clasping his left forearm, his breathing ragged. Typewriter keys clicked. He hesitated, but pain was changing the air around him to waves.[1]

We see here how the verb "had" rolls us into a past event. Notice, too, how quickly within the flashback the sentences return to past tense, and what was the past becomes the new story present.

THE HINGE

Elements of story craft are often likened to elements of housing construction like beams, rooms and windows. Let's follow this familiar comparison and meet our second flashback technique that may be less familiar: the hinge.[2]

Imagine a door hinge. Unlike the decorative hinges at Biltmore, the hinges in my house are plain fellows. They wear no ornate scrollwork. But they get the job done. Holding both the door and the frame with eight screws, they let my front door open while the door remains—I'm relieved to say—attached to the house. We need the same humble-yet-vital invention that connects flashback to story.

In story craft, a hinge is a repeated object or action that moves readers into and out of a flashback.

Film directors use this technique often. In *Cinderella Man,* a movie about boxing champion James J. Braddock (Russell Crowe), director Ron Howard pans to a bedroom dresser where the boxer is setting his watch and rings. Other objects on the dresser—a doily, an opulent jewelry box—hint at family wealth. The camera pans away from the dresser, the screen darkens, and then the camera returns to the dresser. It's the same dresser, but something tells us that times have changed. The opulent items have vanished.[3] The Great Depression has arrived and altered the boxer's life. In this scene, the dresser top works like a hinge.

In *Deepening Fiction,* instructors Sarah Stone and Ron Nyren introduce the hinge using an example from Alice Munro's "Oh, What Avails." Munro repeats a pair of eyeglasses as a hinge. Her lines read: "He was a solid looking boy of about fifteen . . . wearing glasses with one dark lens."[4]

We're led into the story's past and learn why this boy has one dark lens. As the flashback readies to return to the story's present time, Munro intentionally employs a synonym for "dark" and repeats the word "lens" to build this similar phrase: "a smoky lens."[5]

The repeated image of the eyeglasses and the word "lens" becomes the hinge, which helps us move from story present to flashback to story present again.

To make time travel fluid, we can use the past perfect tense "had" plus the hinge.

By the way, we can use other verb changes, too, to signal time slips. In the nonfiction essay, "On Leaving Florida" Marjorie Sanders signals return to the story now with present tense verbs: "There is in the air over Newnans Lake this June day, the faint hush of a test being administered."[6] And with that change of tense, she returns her readers to the anecdote with which she began her essay.

THE MEMORY BLUR

Science fiction film *Arrival* surprises viewers with its nonlinear narrative. Scenes move through time with soft cues. A hinge may be the warmly lit profile of Dr. Louise Banks (Amy Adams) or her lake house window.

In the film's conclusion, though, time-jumbled scenes flow past like a flooded river. Time change becomes fluid, without hinges. An evening meadow with helicopters lifting, Dr. Banks holding an infant and cooing, Dr. Banks spelling with a child, the lake house window, meadow and helicopters, Dr. Banks with the child once more.[7]

Can we writers also blur time change? Can we create fluid shifts in memory?

Although we can't lean on visual cues like films, we can use two tools: verb changes and sentence deconstruction. Let's call this technique "The Memory Blur."

In a key scene, I wanted to stream images within the mind of my character Matthew Goodman and wondered how. How could I blur story present with character memory?

I began to tinker. Instead of using the hinge, I messed around with verb change by using gerunds (verb + -ing) in the flashbacks and by deconstructing sentences into run-ons and fragments. Here is the scene:

> Swim area ropes loomed ahead. Goodman ducked and surfaced, resuming the freestyle while far off, boat engines whined.
>
> Gray eyes, her gray eyes, partially eclipsed by lashes, reflecting two white spots from the recessed lighting, yes, she was standing close in the office, tugging his tie, her hair, her lips parting into a smile, into a one-dimple smile. Trish. Warmth surged through him. The board meeting, right, the board meeting hall of fame and yesterday, just yesterday, touching her skin, tacky from the afternoon outdoors, soft; her hair, softer, his fingers itching, his body—
>
> What had he done?[8]

Gerunds and fragments let me stream images as fluidly, I hope, as the compelling conclusion to the film *Arrival*.

BRAIN MATTER

Apply It: This chapter examines messing with verb change, hinges and sentence construction to move our readers through story time. Practice using the hinge or the memory blur in a scene.

Chapter 16

REVISION TOOLS

For some of us, a bulldozer depicts how we move through the revision process. Instead of a thoughtful strategy, we may try to solve every possible problem in one round or try to edit everything in one sweep: spelling, focus, development, pace, punctuation, diction, characterization, sentence length, setting, conflict, placement of plot points, specificity, etc. This, I'm sorry to say, was my approach for years.

Until I refined my revision process for long projects, I would move through revision feeling overwhelmed. And that wasn't the worst of it. Unfortunately, I also was revising only to my strengths while allowing my weaknesses to persist. My blind spots had blinded me.

So, if the bulldozer method ain't best, are there other strategies to use? There are. Several.

We're going to explore three strategies that best the bulldozer: scene cards, Stein's Triage and the revision checklist.

But first, let's arm ourselves for revision by examining how an editor differentiates levels of revision.

> ## "Revision is like careful carpentry."
> JANET BURROWAY,
> WRITING FICTION

Publishers and editors use highly specific labels for the editing process. We would expect no less. Two particular terms guide the editor's task. "Global revisions" refers to the large issues; it's also called "macro-editing." The focus on smaller issues like grammar and punctuation is called "local revisions" or "micro-editing."

Often a developmental editor is tasked with the global revisions while a copyeditor focuses on local revisions.

How can this knowledge of two editing categories aid our revision? One important way is by first attending the larger issues while initially ignoring picky mechanical details. This lets us prioritize first things first. Then the more finished the story, the more able we are to drop into the polishing work of copyediting, or local revisions.

By prioritizing global and local revisions, we can use one or more of the three strategies to implement smarter and more writer-friendly revising approaches.

GLOBAL REVISIONS	LOCAL REVISIONS
Content	Grammar
Scene structure	Punctuation
Plot	Readability/flow
POV	Pacing

SCENE CARDS: ORDER OUT OF CHAOS

When we, especially pantsers like me, try to order our 386-page manuscript, we may struggle to hold our story whole. So, what tool can help order subplots or show needless scenes or repetitive opening lines?

Scene cards.

This tool involves recording vital scene information on index cards or stick-it notes. Many an author uses the latter and has covered walls with them.

Global Revision Benefits of Scene Cards

- Catch repetitive openings, characters, scenes
- Give visual check to "stage time" per character
- Ease process for reordering scenes
- Show plot holes and plot points

Novelist Tracy Groot (*Madman, The Sentinels of Andersonville, The Maggie Bright*) has a practiced approach with using scene cards. Once she drafts a hundred pages, Groot starts recording scene cards, a method used by other notable writers, including Lamott.

Groot explains, "I've found value using these cards in so many ways."[1] Scene cards allow her to round out scenes, check for multiple types of repetition and reorder information easily.

On her colored index cards, Groot pencils in three types of information: viewpoint characters (coded by the card color), logistical information and scene content.

To start a card, she picks the assigned color for the scene's viewpoint character. Color-coding gives her a quick visual check on how much one character shows up. Does she need to break up a clump of scenes involving one character? Recording the first and last sentences allows Groot to catch repetitive opening lines.[2]

Groot's Scene Cards

1. Top: chapter number, scene pages, scene card number
2. Mid-card: scene's first sentence and summary
3. Bottom: the scene's last sentence

This idiosyncratic use of scene cards guides Groot in her revision. She returns to this tool often.

Writer Sarah Domet suggests another approach in her *Writer's Digest* article "Outlining: Choosing the Best Outline Method for You." Domet recommends recording the scene's setting, characters, scene goal and plot points.

Domet's Scene Cards

1. Setting
2. Characters
3. Scene goals
4. Plot points

Although Domet differs in her approach by noting the setting and the scene's goal, she receives the same benefits as Groot. Domet says, "[A scene card] visually breaks the novel into mini compartments, which makes it easy to see how your story is progressing, how to transition from scene to scene and what might be missing."[3]

The beauty of this tool is how we can shape it to our needs. When I use scene cards, I add another quick visual: color-coded stickers to signify anything from "revise" or "move" to "great job."

Even the back of the index cards can serve us. I jot questions like, "Want to stay with this subplot?" Questions are no longer buried in the pages of my manuscript.

Scene cards are a brilliant tool for global revisions. They further our process by helping us avoid the bulldozer approach.

BRAIN MATTER

Apply It: To get the feel of using scene cards, fill out three index cards, following either Groot's or Domet's approach—or some hybrid that serves your goals. What benefit do you see?

"The biggest difference between a writer and a would-be writer is their attitude toward rewriting."
SOL STEIN,
STEIN ON WRITING

STEIN'S TRIAGE

In the book for fiction and nonfiction writers, *Stein on Writing,* famous editor Sol Stein explains his revision process, which he likens to battlefield triage.

Stein suggests that writers—like medics in the war zone—tend the most important first by using this global-to-local revision approach.[4]

Focus 1: Examine Characters

Stein coaches us to focus first on our characters. Would we want to vacation with them, he asks, alerting us to how likable our characters are. Does our protagonist come to mind often? Are the antagonists complex and interesting? Is there something likable about even them? Is there something unique about our minor characters?[5]

Focus 2: Examine Conflict

Next Stein invites us to ponder our story's central conflict. Is it important? Credible?[6]

Focus 3: Examine Scenes

With a strategy that can grow objectivity about our writing, Stein suggests we determine which scene is our best and then use it to measure all other scenes.[7] Then begin to cut what isn't necessary.

Focus 4: Examine Motive

One last global move: consider cause and effect. Does story action arise from credible motives and responses? Do character actions lift from plausible reasons?[8]

Focus 5: Examine Local Revisions

In this final stage, Stein ushers us into local revisions. He narrows our focus to wordiness and the "between the scenes" filler, which this famous editor exhorts us to cut.[9]

BRAIN MATTER

Write It: Complete Stein's Focus 1 for your story. What do you notice? Move to a second focus and apply it.

REVISION CHECKLIST

In the movie *Sully,* about the US Airways pilot who landed a commercial plane on the Hudson River, we see the pilot (Tom Hanks) and his copilot (Aaron Eckhart) move through a long and detailed chart on their clipboard.[10]

There's a good reason why pilots move through that preflight checklist multiple times daily—right?

Now consider this: what gifts does an external checklist give us writers? Why bother with recording what we know we must examine? An external checklist exists outside of our brain and reminds us what to examine. A checklist prods us to look beyond our strengths and truly examine our blindspots.

We need this—often desperately—as we try to shift from being an overly subjective reader to a more objective one. A checklist also serves us in another way. Remember that bulldozer? A revision agenda coaches us to focus on one thing at a time.

For example, as I moved through my bulldozer method, I revised to my strengths again and again—but had forgotten that little detail called "setting." Now setting is on my revision checklist as well as other items that I might otherwise overlook. For example, does character Trish enter and leave a room or scene with the same props? Do I introduce the setting in the first lines of every new scene? By checking craft elements in a focused way, we can improve our weak areas and maintain our strengths.

These three revision tools can reinforce our sense of control over our manuscripts and grant us an improved method of ordering the chaos.

BRAIN MATTER

Review It: Explain how Stein's Triage differs from the revision checklist. What do they have in common?

Apply It: Create your revision checklist with at least five areas of craft that challenge you (e.g., competing scripts in dialogue, consistent props in scenes, set the scene).

SECTION V

Conversations from the Deep

Chapter 17

GOD TALK, PART I

Pew Research Center asserts that 83 percent of Americans believe in God.[1] Although the survey includes belief across the spectrum—from an impersonal higher power to the personal God of Moses, regardless, 83 percent is a lot of belief. Which might make a new set of questions worth pondering.

First, does the existence of a higher power or God have an impact on what we write and why? And if we're creating characters or writing a life story, how might we make the spiritual realm authentic?

While not all value such questions, some of us do. The next two chapters suggest ways to enliven the spiritual realm.

WRITING MISSIONALLY OR FORMATIONALLY

A continuum can illuminate how writers of faith answer these questions differently: How do we talk about spirituality in a plausible way? Do we even need to? Does writing as a person of faith mean that we need to preach, mention evangelical terms, offer the plan of salvation or simply show sensitivity to the moral universe?

On one end of the continuum, we have the missional writer; on the other, the formational. Where we are on the continuum is determined by our upbringing, denominational preferences, convictions and choices.

This continuum shows us the wide scope of faith responses:[2]

The Missional Writer
- The highest goal is to convert or persuade.
- Likely to utilize direct conversations or dialogue about faith.
- Believers ought to write persuasively about faith.

The Formational Writer
- The highest goal is to show the process of change.

- Likely to utilize indirect conversations or dialogue about faith.
- Believers ought to write authentically about life and/or faith.

This continuum lets us see that people of faith may disagree about what it means to be a believer who writes and better understand where disagreements arise.

Francine Rivers, who has found great success in novels for religious publishers, may tend toward the missional camp. On her website, she differentiates between Christians who write and Christian writers, and says that the latter are "called to present a story that is all about Jesus."[3] While she is careful to say not all people of faith must adhere to this focus, she says, "The purpose of Christian fiction is to whet readers' appetites for a closer relationship with Jesus."[4] Her words alert us to how vital she sees the direct conversations being.

Middle-grade novelist and Newbery winner Dr. Gary D. Schmidt, a person of faith, may fall into the formational camp. When asked how he writes spiritually plausible characters, he says, "Let a character arrive at a new awareness."[5] Here in the formational camp, we encounter the sense of process.

Like Schmidt, thriller novelist Davis Bunn stands in the formational camp. In *The Making of a Christian Bestseller,* Bunn says, "As Christians, we are called to be salt and light in the world. . . . It is required of us to follow God's commands, but does this mean we must write overtly Christian, evangelical-toned stories? To me the answer is no."[6]

A thought-provoking question that writer Hannah VanKampen asks is this: "Can we use evil itself to show the dangers of evil?"[7] In VanKampen's story, a traumatized character turns vampire and devolves into hate and murder. Might a character's darkness also give evidence of light?

"Whether these texts mention God directly or not— and many profoundly religious works, like the Book of Esther, do not—these works strive to present human dilemmas in their full roundness. . . . Almost relentlessly they are concerned with the search for truth."

SHADOW & LIGHT

BRAIN MATTER

Consider It:

1. Which camp do you relate to the most, the missional or the formational camp? Explain.
2. How does being a spiritual person or a person of faith affect the specifics of your writing and/or how you go about writing?
3. In this intersection of being a person of faith and a writer, what is your greatest fear or concern?

MOVIE RATINGS & OUR WRITING

Depending on our faith, generation and upbringing, we will bring certain convictions to our writing about behavior or morals. Letting movie ratings be our guide may help us locate and categorize the level of explicitness in our story.

The American Motion Picture Association uses these familiar categories as part of the movie rating system—a system that's always in flux:

- General Admission (G)
- Parental Guidance (PG)
- Parental Guidance (PG-13)
- Restricted (R)
- NC-17 (formerly X)

These ratings assess the amount that is shown of the following categories: violence, substance abuse, profanity, sexual content and nudity. As you review the movie rating system, which rating would you say your writing earns?

If you are seeking publication, know that your publisher, whether secular or religious, may have strong opinions about including or excluding profanity, violence and sexual content. Publishers often explain their editorial standards on their website. Be aware that your level of explicitness will open or close doors with certain publishers.

But as a writer, especially in the early stages of a work, you need to be free from worrying about who might or might not publish you. What is important now is for you as a writer to evolve as you ponder an ethic for your work.

BRAIN MATTER

Consider It: In categories from violence to sexual content, what do you include—and why? Explore this area without initial judgment. Ponder the following:

Profanity

- What are the reasons to include profanity?
- Is including profanity condoning profanity?
- Are there boundaries that you sense? Describe.

Violence

- What are the reasons to include violence?
- How detailed will the violence be?

Human Sexuality

- How do you as a spiritual person write about sexual conduct?
- Is there such a thing as verbal pornography? Explain. Are there boundaries? If so, describe.

CRAFT MOVES FOR PLAUSIBLE SPIRITUALITY

For those of us who want to touch on spiritual elements—whether we write for religious or secular markets—we will likely wonder how we can portray spirituality in a meaningful and authentic way.

These story craft suggestions explain how.

Avoid Religious Jargon

Use common language. Religious people—and nonreligious—understand well the simple triad of faith, hope and love. But once we employ Christianese or theological terms, we've lost readers beyond our immediate circles.

Example: Donald Miller's memoir, *Blue Like Jazz.* Miller determined to limit religious language while he explored spiritual epiphanies.

Use Brief Competing Scripts

Use brief touches of dialogue with competing scripts. As your characters talk faith, tap Stein's powerful tool of competing scripts, where each character desires something different. Let sparks fly!

Example: *Salmon Fishing in the Yemen* (film). A Yemeni prince gently tutors a British scientist in matters of faith. (See YouTube, "Salmon Fishing in the Yemen Man of Faith.")

Unfold Epiphany

Orchestrate an epiphany. Or, as Schmidt says, "Let the character come into a new awareness."[8] The epiphany requires verbal tools like our Hitchcockian close-up, symbols and metaphors.

Example: In the short story "Pigeon Feathers," Updike uses poetic intensifiers to convey an epiphany.

Play Against Type

Don't just avoid stereotypical characters. Offer a character who subverts expectations.

Example: Sandra Bullock playing Leigh Anne Tuohy in *The Blind Side*. Despite its evident Christian themes, this movie enjoyed immense popularity. Perhaps because Mrs. Tuohy—the kind lady who helped a homeless kid—was full of sass. She was no "church lady."

BRAIN MATTER

Review It: For one or more of these craft tools, think of a good example from your reading or movie viewing. Which of these craft moves may serve your story?

Write It: Practice two craft moves as you create dialogue between teenagers of differnt faiths.

Chapter 18

GOD TALK, PART II

We struggle to name what is so about the universe—this shadow of something or Someone. Fortunately, we have craft tools that help us go deep. Leaning on nature, symbols and certain genres can facilitate conversations about invisible realities.

> ## "The spiritual world is hidden and perfectly revealed in the physical world."
>
> ### Richard Rohr

Deepening with Nature

Actor Harrison Ford, most famous for his role as Han Solo in the *Star Wars* series, says nature set him to thinking about a divine being. In a *Parade* magazine interview, he attributed this awareness to his 800-acre Wyoming ranch. "I'd purchased land and had a sense of stewardship about the place, because the majesty of nature is so apparent there. . . . I had a sense of awe, a sense that nature is so complex and fascinating that it's as close as I've come to understanding the notion of divinity."[1] Ford's words remind us how nature can lift our awareness of something beyond.

The opening chapters of Romans hint that something of the divine is known through nature. The book of Psalms, many of them written by an outdoors-guy-turned-king, includes verse after verse of nature metaphor or allusion. The prophets also allude to objects in nature like the stars and what they can tell us about God.

Flannery O'Connor is the go-to writer for using the tool of nature as a God-presence. In her short story "Revelation," through personification, nature responds to the self-righteous and angry Mrs. Turpin and leads her to a spiritual epiphany.

In the following excerpt, Mrs. Turpin is perhaps having her first real conversation with God. She pelts God with a question. And then, she receives an answer:

The color of everything, field and crimson sky, burned for a moment with a transparent intensity. The question carried over the pasture and across the highway and the cotton field and returned to her clearly like an answer from beyond the wood.[2]

The land and sky reveal something to this shattered character. Mrs. Turpin senses a presence in nature that alters her.

In *Everything Belongs,* Catholic priest Richard Rohr says, "This world is the hiding place of God and the revelation of God."[3] Rohr's words remind us of the "phenomenon of presence." Nature functions in literature and beyond as a powerful tool of spiritual revelation.

DEEPENING WITH SYMBOLS

Along with using nature to deepen our spiritual conversation, another literary tool lets us keep our stories from being merely puddle-deep: symbols.

Water appears to be a prevalent symbol in my novel, *The Surface of Water,* although I didn't consciously cultivate this symbol, and its title was late arriving. Instead, this symbol emerged as part of the "beyondness" of writing—those moments in our writing that arise from our intuitive or subconscious self.

Trust the beyondness and its fruit. Then do some tending.

Early on, Matthew Goodman, a fifty-five-year-old megachurch pastor, washes his hands and notices how the water feels. He observes "how you can touch it, but not hold it . . . like Someone else he knew."[4] I wasn't working at linking God to water, but Goodman's thoughts did. He longs for swimming—perhaps a metaphor of grace for him—but for now, water is something that he only allows to touch a small part of himself.

In the ending, Matthew plunges into Lake Michigan to commit suicide and swims beyond the safety ropes where, now submerged in "grace," he finally encounters God.

If I wanted to heighten the symbolic meaning, I could add more metaphors and similes or use quotations from the Gospels where grace is compared to water—something Pastor Goodman would plausibly think.

MFA professor Bruce Holland Rogers suggested other possible ways of gleaning this symbol: "A starting place might be to keep a little diary of water, catching your thoughts about water across many days, just as a reminder that you are looking for more ways to think about water. And looking up some of those remarkable physical characteristics of water might be worth your time, too."[5]

Taking what the beyondness of writing gives us, the symbols, and emphasizing them can deepen the spiritual conversation.

BRAIN MATTER

Consider It: What recurring symbols or aspects of nature do you find in your story? Or is something coming to mind that you could integrate?

DEEPENING WITH GENRE

A third tool that can create an authentic spiritual realm is telling our stories in a spiritual-friendly genre like magical realism or fantasy.

Magical realism makes the invisible realm visible; it sets the miraculous into ordinary life. For example, in the Christmas classic, *It's a Wonderful Life,* despondent George Bailey (Jimmy Stewart) interacts with his guardian angel Clarence. While everyone else in Bedford Falls believes George crazy for talking to someone they can't see or hear, we know that Clarence is real. So real, in fact, that his actions save his ward—and earns Clarence his wings.

Or take the previously mentioned film *Levity.* Here the store clerk murdered years ago by protagonist Manuel Jordan (Billy Bob Thorton) appears to the latter and aids self-forgiveness and redemption. Like *It's a Wonderful Life,* we understand that only Manuel sees the ghostly clerk.

Novelist Louise Erdrich lets the spiritual realm permeate *The Last Report on the Miracles at Little No Horse.* An early example of magical realism happens when character Agnes DeWitt awakens in a cabin after near-drowning. She finds herself warm and cared for by a stranger. When she awakens the next morning, the room and bed that she believed she had seen are gone. The stranger, gone. She deems it a miracle, that God cared for her. Within the story's reality, this is the truth.[6]

Fantasy, unlike magical realism, creates a less explicit and a more formational spiritual conversation through its use of broad strokes: good versus evil, light versus dark. Which may explain its immense popularity. Through fantasy we understand and experience enormous intuitive truths.

Nature. Symbols. Genre. These three tools can deepen our stories by helping us convey authentic spirituality.

BRAIN MATTER

Ponder It: What stories come to your mind that use nature, symbols or genre to deepen the spiritual conversation? Which tool may deepen your story?

SECTION VI

Junk Drawer

Chapter 19

IN RELATION TO SELF

Post-it notes. Tape. Sharpies. Item after item jostles together in my kitchen junk drawer, and despite the name "junk," these articles are anything but.

Like a junk drawer, this chapter offers writers common and useful tools.

ARTISTIC MISSION STATEMENTS

West Michigan oil painter and illustrator Jim Connelly is a true believer—in artistic mission statements. A few years ago, he crafted a statement that named his artistic aim. "As an artist," he wrote, "I humbly pursue the godly excellence I see in creation by practicing my craft daily with energy and reverence for the gift God has given me."[1]

He also described himself as a "creative impressionistic painter with the ability to draw expressively and accurately."[2]

For a time, Connelly read his statement aloud daily, and then his art—and his opportunities—began to change. New doors opened, including a prestigious cover for *Southwestern Art*. Soon after, he challenged me as a writer to craft my own statement.

I followed Connelly's two-part structure, confirming why I write and explaining who I am as a writer. I also brainstormed words I love like "soul" and "truth." After opening with my commitment to God, my statement reads, "I am a creative wordsmith with the ability to reflect and reveal the human soul and its need for God truthfully and redemptively. My unique combination of depth, experience, insight and word use makes my work a personal statement about my fervent belief in God and his love for us."

Writing this statement stirred my inner fire, my desire to write. It propelled me forward.

Roy Peter Clark also recommends writing a mission statement for projects. In *Writing Tools,* he suggests this example: "I want to portray my protagonist as a fully human character, not some cardboard cut-out saint."[3] Clark adds, "Most writers aspire to some invisible next step—for a story or a body of work. Writing down your mission turns your vague hopes into language."[4]

Like oil painter Jim Connelly, I now read my artistic mission statement aloud. It has become a ladder for me, a step forward, a plank on which I balance.

BRAIN MATTER

Write It: Draft your artistic mission statement. First, list words that matter to you (e.g., "authentic"). Then shape your list into a paragraph. Print your mission statement and hang it in view. Empower yourself by reading it aloud daily for one week.

WRITING AS BURDEN

Sometimes being a writer is difficult. Perhaps part of the challenge arises because of the truth we must disclose to ourselves or others.

WRITER IN A BULLETPROOF VEST

Contributed by Iris Graville[5]

Almost ten years ago, I got hooked on *Castle,* a television series about New York Police Department (NYPD) detectives. Cop shows don't usually appeal to me, but in this one, main character Rick Castle was a mystery novelist with writer's block. When the NYPD questioned him in connection with a series of murders that imitated crime scenes in his books, Castle found inspiration in Detective Kate Beckett.

Castle pulled some strings with a friend in the mayor's office to follow Beckett and her fellow detectives in their crime-solving in order to revive his writing.

Before going out on a case, Beckett would slide a gun into a holster slung low on her waist and strap on a black bulletproof vest; bold white letters marched across her back, POLICE. Castle wore a vest, too. The letters on his, WRITER.

As much as she hates to admit it, Beckett depends on Castle's writer intuition to anticipate moves the criminals she's tracking might make. She accepts Castle's presence but, with his lack of police training, she fears for his safety; they usually encounter murderers or armed robbers when they're on a case. She insists on the bulletproof vest.

I want one of those vests to wear when I sit at my writing desk. Popular advice to writers goes something like, "Writing is easy. Just sit down at a typewriter and open a vein." That sounds dramatic, but putting my beliefs and experiences into words on paper can seem as risky as when Castle slinks around an abandoned warehouse.

When I sit down to write, I'm not exposing myself to criminals' weapons, but I am opening myself to feelings that can rip through me with the near-force of a bullet or knife blade. When I'm present to the source of my writing, I encounter beliefs, memories, truths, grief and joy that can leave me gasping for breath or choking on tears.

I know there's no gun aimed at my chest when I write, no actual possibility of physical harm. Yet my heart races and my mouth turns cottony as if I were being pursued by some danger.

What is it I fear?

When I'm writing my truth, I have to go to those deep, tender places within. To the places where I reveal my weaknesses and flaws. Where I expose my faithlessness, my desire to be in control, my fears that others will reject me if I share my true self or that they'll disagree with what I hold dear.

In *To Be Broken and Tender,* Quaker author Marge Abbott writes of how she sees the Divine "at work in the hearts of individuals so that they are tender to the pain of the world and the selfish power of the ego is broken apart." The process of writing opens me and makes me tender to my own pain and the pain of others. My heart may be broken open as I seek to find the words. My ego may be broken as the essence I call God works in me.

Abbott cautions, "Bringing the painful into the Light does take courage and can open many wounds." When I write, I often access feelings and knowledge I didn't know I had or that I'd ignored. I awaken memories of hurting, fear or sadness that I've buried so deep in my unconscious, the pain can feel like a punch in the gut. That's the depth I want to get to in my writing, to those places where the memory and the knowing are alive, touchable. But I ache as I open my heart, and my tender spots need protection, the shielding of a bulletproof vest.

I could keep my beliefs and awarenesses private. I could, and have, kept them locked deep inside to avoid self-judgment or criticism. But when I write from my center, I know that I'm carried by the spirit that wants me to use and develop my gifts as a writer, that loves me no matter what I put on the page, that yearns for me to tend to myself and others through writing. Isn't that knowledge my bulletproof vest?

> The sky outside my window this morning is gray. Fog cuts off the tops of the trees and hangs over the bay like a false ceiling hiding a higher one. Somewhere—above that layer of fog—the sun, the light, is shining. I venture toward my desk aware of the love within me and around me, protecting those tender and broken places waiting to be opened.

STORY AS BURDEN

Zane Grey, considered one of America's best Western writers, penned the novel, *The Vanishing American,* about horrific reservation conditions in the 1920s for Native Americans. The worst offenders? Missionaries and agency workers. Atrocious abuse—financial profiteering to rape—occurred at their hands.

This novel has a Navajo as viewpoint character and protagonist. Nophaie is educated in white schools before returning to the reservation where he witnesses the abuse of his people.

In this excerpt from Grey's 1922 diary, we read why he felt compelled to write this story:

> I am writing my Indian story.... It is a responsibility, this novel. The Indian story has never been written. Maybe I am the man to do it. I must go deeper and even stronger into my treasure mine and stint nothing of time, toil, or torture.[6]

Little did Grey foresee how torturous the journey involving *The Vanishing American* would be.

The story began encountering enormous protest after *Ladies Home Journal* serialized Grey's novel. Readers and church leaders bombarded the magazine editors over the negative depiction of the missionaries.

As a result, the book publishers refused to print the novel the way Grey had written it. Instead, changes were required: don't let the Native American protagonist marry his sweetheart—she is white, after all. Also, eliminate or soften the depiction of missionaries.

But Grey had done his homework. What he wrote was happening. Some missionaries or posers had arrived to abuse the poverty-ridden natives. Apparently, though, to the decision-makers, only the reader complaints mattered.

The publishers insisted and Grey acquiesced. He altered his story, which cost him. In a letter to his publishers, he laments:

This is the first time in my life that I have been driven away from the truth, from honor and ideals, and in this case, from telling the world of the tragedy of the Indian. . . . I wonder what effect it will have upon me.[7]

Grey also was pressured to destroy the original manuscript. His son, however, knowing his father, believed that Grey had saved it. Sure enough, after Grey's death, Loren Grey found the manuscript and published it in 1982.

Nearly six decades later, the novel appeared as it ought.

Other stories abound of writers struggling to tell their truth and meeting sharp resistance or censorship.

Charlotte Brontë's nineteenth-century classic *Jane Eyre* depicts the harsh conditions of private boarding schools—conditions that in 1840s England included insufficient food and clothing, long marches in icy weather, public humiliation as a discipline tool and even death.

Brontë knew these conditions firsthand. Her two oldest sisters, Maria and Elizabeth, died at Cowan Bridge, a boarding school, likely from tuberculosis. What Brontë witnessed appears in *Jane Eyre*. Cowan Bridge School becomes Haworth, and headmaster Rev. William Carus-Wilson becomes the hated Mr. Robert Brocklehurst.

According to journalist Ian Herbert, the success of the novel lifted the account of Haworth to Carus-Wilson, who threatened to sue Brontë.[8] In an exchange of letters, Brontë narrowly avoided suit by issuing an apology and by sending Carus-Wilson a revised section with permission to publish.[9]

A century later, Newbery-winner Madeleine L'Engle also suffered for her international bestselling, *A Wrinkle in Time*.

Reporter Steve Hendrix writes that at first, publisher after publisher rejected it. One editor called it "bewildering" while another said it carried a devil.[10] Then once it was published, it was frequently banned. Some said it was "too Christian" while others charged it with maligning Christianity.

A Wrinkle in Time has been in print since 1962. It has sold over 10 million copies, says Hendrix. And yet, it cost its writer. "Each rejection . . . is a wound," L'Engle journaled.[11]

These famous authors, Grey, Brontë and L'Engle, were faithful to the story that came to them—and suffered. Might we find ourselves also suffering for our stories?

BRAIN MATTER

Write It:

1. In what ways might your writing journey cost you? In what ways might your particular story cost you?
2. What may signal to you that your story is worth paying the cost?

Chapter 20

IN RELATION TO OTHERS

"Writing troubles every writer I know," says *Catch-22* author Joseph Heller.[1] Even those who love it. Getting ideas. Believing in ourselves. Carving out time. Contacting editors. Withstanding the inevitable no. Writing isn't for the faint of heart. Finding other writers, I believe, is a must.

WRITING GROUPS

A writing group can give us needed accountability and fuel. But how do we find one and then if we do, what do we do next?

Finding a Group

- Post a note at a local bookstore, church or library.
- Contact local English professors or conferences.
- Use postings on Facebook or other social media.

Making a Group

In *The Writer's Market,* writer John Moir suggests the following in making a good match with fellow writers:

- Match purposes.
- Compare genre types, goals and skill levels.
- Push yourself to join groups beyond your level.[2]

Figuring Group Logistics

Size: The rule of thumb in group work is five to ten participants. Beyond ten, the group can become unwieldy.

Attendance: Groups run from once a week to once a month.

Choosing Type of Writing Group

Writing groups, like horses, come in many different types. Groups usually fall, though, into either critique groups or non-critique groups.

> "At first, the thought of getting feedback
> from people who don't know me was a little
> frightening, but working with the group has been
> invigorating—like an early morning stretch after
> crawling out of bed."
>
> REBECCA WOLFE,
> THE WELL PARTICIPANT

Type 1: The Critique Group

A critique group offers members feedback. A good critique group can supply just what we need: a reader's take on our writing.

Strengths

- Opportunity to improve craft
- Opportunity to network

Weaknesses

- Unpredictable quality of feedback
- Potential for destructive criticism

Critique groups may flounder when one (or more) member changes into The Critic who contemptuously blasts others. The Critic employs blanket statements like "This wasn't very good" instead of helpful specifics like "Starting with a personal story would have increased my interest." Their goal isn't to help, but to disrupt or destroy.

Confront a member one-on-one who is sliding toward The Critic, and if the spirit doesn't change, prune them from the group. A toxic member can destroy a group's atmosphere, trust and confidence.

Critique groups go about business in numerous ways. Here is one approach:

Before Group

- Email group members an agreed amount of pages (10-20 pages double-spaced).
- Record responses to strengths and weaknesses.

During Group

- Start with a check in: How is the writing going?
- Next, members discuss comments, avoiding directly addressing the writer.
- The writer listens, records feedback and remains quiet until the end to limit defensiveness.
- When comments end, the writer may ask questions for clarification.

Type 2: The Non-Critique Group

Non-critique groups meet regularly to talk writing, soul care and life. They listen. They encourage. They exhort. They spark each other's creativity.

Suggestions for Non-Critique Groups

- Discuss project ideas and news.
- Explore solutions for writing problems, issues.
- Take turns—possibly set time limits.

Groups, as famous rock bands might reveal, can be fraught with difficulty. We are broken people. Some writers avoid groups and have instead only one writing partner. Either way, being connected with and accountable to another writer is, I believe, a must.

WRITING BUDS & THE GIMLET EYE

The Guild—they're my tribe. Ann Byle, Sharron Carrns, Lorilee Craker, Tracy Groot and Alison Hodgson. Together we've traveled through life challenges that include a house fire, the death of parents, financial struggles and the challenge of being a writer. The computer that crashes. The editor or agent who says, "I must see this!" and never replies. The publishing house that insists on an impossible timeline.

We listen to each other's laments. We support each other. We carry each other's dreams. And when we need to speak fiercely into another's life, we do. We apply The Gimlet Eye.

"And you're not writing . . . why?"

"What's one small goal that you can set?"

"Did you contact that editor yet?"

When I was losing ground in contacting agents, Lorilee served up her specialty: proposal surgery. (She's very good and runs a proposal critique business.) Within minutes of our time sipping coffee together, she strengthened my query.

On another day, Lorilee sat near me and looked at me. "Is it possible that you're shrinking?"

Shrinking?

Shrinking was code for what happens when we are saying no to our inner writing prompts. Her words—which may have felt risky for her to say—were perfect. That she spoke into a problem she sensed is the gravel bed of friendship, of companionship, of love itself.

Proverbs wisely includes "the wound of a friend" in its tome.[3] We're not talking about a betrayal here. We're talking about a friend who cares enough to lovingly and fiercely say what needs saying.

Who is better fit as a companion for the writing journey than a writing friend with a gimlet eye?

WRITING BETRAYALS

Old West gunfights. Karate showdowns. Wars and violence and never-ending disputes are part of our world. Might disputes and betrayals also be part of our writing journey?

Unfortunately . . . yes.

A hurtful betrayal happened to me decades ago. It involved an older colleague who talked and listened with excitement about my life. After she retired and moved away, I asked her if I could pay her to edit my novel.

She agreed, so I sent her my manuscript. My hopes zoomed. Would she love it so much that she'd stay up late to read it?

I waited. Of course, it'd take her time. I waited some more. And then her email arrived.

Her email marched across the screen in capital letters. Along my neck, my nerves tingled. Her words shouted, "Your novel is so banal!"

Banal? Who would shout that?

I jumped out of the chair, threw on my coat and walked, walked, walked. Her hateful words blistered. Betrayal. I hadn't seen it. What had I missed about this person?

Soon Cameron's *The Artist's Way* coaxed me to put this woman in my Monster Hall of Fame and to write about my wound.[4] I learned this lesson: anyone who resorts to lava-throwing can be held apart from me.

There are, in fact, spiritual shields and moves to use against those whose goal is to destroy.

I realized this person, whom I mistook as a friend, had harmed me. And worse, she wanted to harm me. Did I need to let her stop me? No. I could heal. I could learn tactics to protect myself and my writing.

Could I also trust those who are trustworthy? I could. Not all betray.

But the betrayer? I took her at her word. I didn't plead my case or push. Instead, I let her go. I would never entrust my creativity to her again.

BRAIN MATTER

Consider It:

1. We can betray ourselves by not writing, by showing our writing too early or to a toxic person. Where does your self-betrayal show up?
2. Have you experienced betrayal in your writing? Explain the situation. Now draw a caricature of the person as a monster.[5]

Chapter 21
THE WRITING VOCATION

"Way leads on to way," warns poet Robert Frost in his well-known, "The Road Not Taken."[1] A chosen path carries with it its own momentum and with its direction, more choices than we first might think.

The moment we decide to write for others and not only ourselves, we begin to encounter many other decisions and possibilities. Because writing attaches deeply to our core, these decisions often trigger fear and glitchy behavior. *Go to a writing conference? Me? Try to get published? What am I thinking!*

However, Frost's poem doesn't only warn. It also encourages. Its last lines remind us that taking the uncommon path gives us an uncommon life.

WRITING CONFERENCES

Attend writing conferences. Yes, despite resistance. Despite fear. Despite crowds of people. Attend.

Writing conferences serve us in numerous ways. Attending strengthens our courage—although our first one can be *very* disruptive. Conferences help us to step into the professional side of writing. Their classes inform our craft. They also help us network where agents, editors and other writers gather. Many conferences offer what is often called "one-on-ones," where an attendee gets the enormous gift of speaking with a professional for ten minutes. Perhaps ironically, too, the act of spending money for our writing can cement our resolve.

Prepare for Attending

- Map out session preferences: what do you need now? An agent, or a discussion on first lines?
- Go with a buddy. If that's not possible, go and make a new buddy.
- Know that many attendees are introverts who are really, really scared.

One writing friend, Shari Dragovich, pushes herself each year to go somewhere new. She's adamant about not allowing her comfort zone to control her. One year she attended a local Virginia conference; another year, she chose faraway Alaska.

WRITING RETREATS

Writing retreats, unlike conferences, offer more advanced writers something other than craft instruction. Retreats offer writers creative space to write or workshop—that is, getting pages of work critiqued. Retreats often become the next step for conference-experienced writers.

An example of a wonderful retreat is the Harvester Island Wilderness Workshop hosted by Leslie Leyland Fields. Set on an island near Kodiak, writers workshop—and watch whales.

PUBLISHING BASICS

So, you've decided to step toward publishing. Now what? Here's a common route toward accomplishing this mission.

STEPS TO PUBLISHING

1. Draft a story; revise.
2. Study story craft.
3. Attend writing conferences.
4. Get comments from writing group.
5. Revise. Revise. Revise.
6. Get comments from beta readers   and/or hire an editor; revise.
7. Write proposal; revise proposal.
8. Query agents or editors.
9. Build platform. Revise.
10. Wait a year; you're published.

TRADITIONAL PUBLISHING

Publishing methods and trends can be compared to a flowing river that curves and changes, waxes and wanes. Publishing changes through the eras. Before we explore new publishing alternatives, let's examine types of traditional publishing available today that range from large to small and secular to religious.

Traditional publishing, what we sometimes think of as publishing proper, grants the familiar perks we expect like an advance, royalties and publicity.

Typical norms for traditional publishing follow:

- Author pays no money to the publisher.
- Publisher pays an advance; once that's earned out, royalties.
- A team of professionals works on project: acquisitions editor, developmental editor, copyeditor, proofreader, graphic designer, marketer/publicist.

Within traditional publishing, there's a dividing line between large publishers and small presses.

Large publishers almost always require an author to be agented. Unless these publishers send acquisitions editors to a writing conference, which can bypass an agent, they don't want authors contacting them. Sending a manuscript to a publisher who hasn't asked for it is called an "unsolicited manuscript" or an "unsolicited submission." This rarely garners a contract.

Most agents and publishing houses won't read unsolicited manuscripts, but they may read a proposal. A proposal is a document with set categories like a story summary, author bio and market analysis. To learn how to write an effective proposal, see *How to Write a Book Proposal* by Jody Rein.

Large publishers have the best distribution system. Thus, authors flock to them. They can get books out. On the downside, these large corporations may not tend the individual well. And the amount of sales determines whether a large publisher keeps an author for a second book or not.

Small traditional publishers differ in that they often don't require an agent. They can offer more author care and input, but will have smaller (or no) advances and, of course, a smaller distribution reach.

Another dividing line in traditional publishing is secular versus religious publishers. An obvious difference would be morality standards. For example, some religious publishers have the Sensitive Reader, someone who becomes a gatekeeper against profanity, explicit sex scenes and violence. A few religious houses also may require an overt salvation plan.

Remember, though, that among religious publishers differences exist. Faith-based publishers like WordFarm allow more edginess and prefer a less missional approach.

NONTRADITIONAL PUBLISHING

The internet tsunami washed ashore and altered the entire coastline of the publishing industry. Why publishing? One phrase, says industry expert Jane Friedman: "on-line retail."[2] In other words, the internet altered book distribution. This changed everything.

The internet—or should we say, Amazon—whisked away the need for maintaining an expensive retail store. Which simplified the life of the self-publisher. Bookstores typically wouldn't carry self-published works, so with the advent of Amazon, selling indie flourished.

Also, the brick-and-mortar investment large publishers made, their overhead, may be driving some of their risk-averse choices, says hybrid and traditional author Delilah Marvelle. She explains in "Making the Choice to Switch," part of *Writer's Digest's Guide to Self-Publishing,* that New York publishers have "created outrageous costs for themselves, like having expensive leases in the most expensive area in the United States."[3] This writer seems to think that high rents might be the tail that now wags some publishers.

Within self-publishing, there are vital distinctions:

- Vanity Press: author doesn't involve publishing professionals and publishes manuscript as is.
- Hybrid Publishing or Indie Publishing: author hires publishing services (e.g., BookBaby).

For a thorough guide to publishing, see Friedman's blogs and books, *Publishing 101* and *The Business of Being a Writer.* For self-publishing, see the *Writer's Digest Guide to Self-Publishing.*

SELF-PUBLISHING:
A VALID OPTION

What finally convinced me in my journey toward indie publishing? Two words: Patti Hill.

Novelist Patti Hill had impressed me at Breathe 2013. I hadn't read Hill, but I saw her in action. Hill knew fiction craft. She was a well-established, agented author whose fiction had placed in the Christy Awards and ALA.

Fast-forward four years. My novel, *The Surface of Water*—an edgy story—garnered interest and rejections again and again. A San Francisco agent wanted to see it—and then said no. This pattern repeated itself multiple times. I struggled to reassure myself. The novel had been through revisions, an MFA program and beta readers.

Then an email from editor Kathleen Kerr perhaps explained the rejections:

Unfortunately, I've got wretched news—this just isn't the sort of novel we are acquiring these days. We're looking for more 'escapist' fiction, and this is a bit too literary for our market. It sounds like a fantastic read, though, and it seems like a brave book, exploring questions that don't always make us comfortable. I encourage you to continue pursuing publication.[4]

Kerr's words encouraged me. "A fantastic read"? "A brave book"? Maybe all the rejections weren't about my writing abilities.

Finally, though, the last straw broke in my pursuit of traditional publishing. A British editor wanted the entire manuscript. My pulverized hope grew. And then the news came. His publishing house announced bankruptcy.

Somehow at that moment, Hill's book *The San Clemente Bait Shop & Telephony* bleeped my radar, so I found it and devoured it. I marveled at Hill's fine craftsmanship—and I was picky. She could tell a quality story. I also liked its edginess. Then with shock, I realized it. Hill had self-published. Why? Because an agented and award-winning author couldn't find a home for her fresh and edgy novel. So, she published it herself.[5]

That spring, Hill won the national LYRA Grand Prize for this novel that nobody seemed to want. It also was a finalist for a Colorado Book Award.

This turned me. And I had been hard to turn. I was a college professor for heaven's sake. I had standards to uphold. I couldn't explain my dogged—perhaps foolish—commitment to my novel. But, if Hill's finely crafted story—with its authentic level of edgy—could be missed, maybe the same was true for mine.

Middle-grade novelist Zetta Elliot suggests another reason for self-publishing: to avoid the sociological problem of publishers acting as gatekeepers. As a minority who, like Hill, found success in traditional publishing, Elliot also was told often by agents and editors that there was no market for her stories that offered minorities as protagonists.[6]

During a Writer's Digest IndieLAB keynote, Elliot referenced Kathleen Horning, director of the Cooperative Children's Book Center (CCBC). Horning compiled 2013 statistics showing that of 650 middle-grade novels with human protagonists, only 14 featured children of color as protagonists.[7] Unfortunately, recent stats continue to echo these findings.

These statistics plus her own discouraging experience led Elliot to conclude that part of her job in self-publishing is "to push back against dominate voices."[8]

So, self-publish? Why not? There may be several rather important reasons to do so.

INDIE UNDEFINED

The term "indie" in movies signals a film done outside the big studios or movie industry corporations. It's outside the mainstream. In the writing world, the word "indie" can signal anything from small publishers to hybrid publishing.

Chapter 22

HIRING AN EDITOR

OK, so I was sulking.

I draped over my couch like an afghan. The writer's magazine I held would soon expire. Finally. Then all those published writers would stop gloating. These fellow writers seemed to sneer at my unfulfilled dreams, but now there was an upside. I'd not be renewing.

I was a longtime English professor who had articles, chapters and a few short stories in print, but in 2003, my first novel manuscript had gotten a no from a Cadillac of an editor. Then many revisions later, more editors pronounced the same verdict. Into the bottom file *Milton's Cloud* went, and I busily started a new manuscript, *The Surface of Water,* only to stall out after the initial drafting and revising.

What was the next step? I didn't know.

My courage and arrogance were fractured. I could no longer determine if my manuscript was ready for an acquisitions editor. Then again, my self-talk reminded me that I had a graduate degree in journalism. Plus, as a professor I annually graded 600 essays and made money on small editing jobs. If I could edit others' work, couldn't I edit my own work to a publishable level? I was not sure anymore that I could. If I didn't dare send the manuscript to a publisher, what was next?

Then, there on the couch, magic happened.

My muse zinged me—not in fairy dust but in Times New Roman font. A one-inch ad lifted off the magazine page:

Award-winning fiction writer, graduate of Iowa Writers' Workshop, creative writing teacher for 35 years, provides personalized manuscript editing. I offer detailed editing, honest evaluation, and sensitive critique. Contact Hugh Cook.

Wow, I thought. *The Hugh Cook?*

In 1990, I had heard Cook at Calvin College's Festival of Faith and Writing. The tall bearded writer exhibited diamond-cut craftsmanship and kindness. I resolved to read this Canadian literary writer. I even started teaching two of his short stories, "A Canadian Education" and "Pisces."

Now I wondered if this could this be him.

I jerked upward from the couch and reached for my laptop. Google listed multiple Hugh Cooks, including one known for science fiction.

Please, God, I thought, *let it be that literary guy.*

The ad's website assured me. Its picture showed the bearded man I admired. I immediately emailed him. I then clicked the send button and noticed something. I wasn't sulking anymore.

The next day brought Cook's reply. In a brief, friendly manner, he explained his editing services and liked our Calvin connection. If I wanted to proceed, he said, please send him a short piece of my writing.

What happened next mattered a great deal.

I did not pause. I did not second-guess myself. I did not allow the Critic to have my ear. Had I listened, I would have heard, "You can't show The Hugh Cook your writing! What? You crazy?"

But show him my writing I did. Thankfully, I did not need to wait long. Again he responded promptly:

Cynthia, just read the chapter. You create the scene very well: Goodman's ex-pectations for the meeting, the breezy old boys' atmosphere, then the tension in the room when Trisha speaks.

I vaulted from the couch to perform an Irish jig. He liked it. Hugh Cook liked my writing!

Breathless, I returned to my laptop and continued reading: "I'm struck by the chapter's prose style—" More compliments were coming. Who wouldn't love my prose style?

—which contains a predominance of short, choppy sentences and a number of deliberate sentence fragments, all of which creates a somewhat herky-jerky effect. Are you deliberately creating this effect to suggest Goodman's confi-dence, almost cockiness?

Gulp. Herky-jerky? My prose? I slumped. A moment later, I gathered my wits and opened my manuscript. The section was a little herky-jerky. In my multiple revisions, I had missed this.

It didn't matter that I was an English professor. It didn't matter that I had a hundred articles in print and had won two short story contests. Putting my writing beneath another's scrutiny made way for this new realization: I really wasn't reading my writing well.

I opened a new email and slowly typed:

Hugh, I understood your feedback to say that the scene was well created— and (hopefully) came to life. However, the style—the use of fragments—felt "herky-jerky." I understood this to mean that I'm overusing a technique and it's interfering with readability. Truth be told, I can't read my writing as someone else can. Are you willing to work with me?

Cook's warm reply was immediate. Yes, he was willing; he even had made a computer file named "Cynthia Beach." A new writing relationship had begun.

The next summer I addressed a box for Hamilton, Ontario. It carried to Cook a stern revision of *The Surface of Water*. Then I waited. I weeded the perennial garden. I checked the mailbox. I groomed my horse. I checked the mailbox. Finally, a battered box from the neighboring country arrived home.

What Cook sent back was priceless.

He told me what was working and what wasn't. He showed me my bad habits that included—horror!—improper verb conjugations.

"It's a worthy story, Cynthia," he said in a four-page letter. His words became new fuel for the journey. If Hugh Cook thought this, I could keep on this story and fix what needed fixing. He touched on all the craft issues from point of view to dialogue. Then Cook finished his letter with a caveat:

This evaluation of your novel is one person's critique, and none of it is gospel truth. Just advice. Anything I say in this evaluation should be evaluated in turn by you. . . . Trust your own instincts for the novel. You have a worthwhile novel here, one that will be even stronger after another rigorous rewrite.

The critique landed like a cat on all fours. I was heartened, energized and clear. I knew the next step. I left my couch and returned to my writing room. The process of being edited showed me the next step. I hadn't time to sulk.

Chapter 23

THE CRAFT OF CRITIQUING

Think surgery: careful hands, a studied approach, effort for the cause. The art of critiquing is the art of surgery. Our writing and another's are holy ground. However imperfect the piece is, someone lovingly labored over it. Approaching writing with reverence serves everyone well. When we approach writing to critique it, we need an inner quiet, not an angry or judgmental attitude.

With those careful hands, we move slowly and patiently over another's work. With that studied approach, we bring along our sturdy skills as readers. (Notice how I didn't say "as editors"? Most of us aren't and may do harm in trying to be.) And why all this effort? We're here to help, to serve, to move another writer forward.

THE CRITIC & THE MUSE

Unfortunately, like a full moon to a werewolf, an invitation to be a critique partner gives some who appear to be normal writers an excuse to turn monster Critic. The person who becomes the Critic is to be avoided. Really. When someone becomes the Critic, he or she loses the right to comment on your writing. Be on guard. This person is destructive and aims to harm the heart of your work—you.

The Critic has a distinct voice. Its tone is angry, contemptuous, dismissive, belittling. You get the message. The Critic will make smothering blanket judgments like "This isn't good."

Who can get out from under that?

Even though a critique must deliver some bad news, there's an important difference between the voice of the Critic and a good critique.

The Critic will . . .

- say general statements like "This is dumb!"
- focus on belittling the story itself (topic, similarities to other stories, etc.).
- omit offering fixable craft observations.

On the other hand, someone who has mastered good critiquing, or the Muse, enters the piece with respect and empathy. This person will offer specific comments such as "The first line pulled me in" or "I can see your character."

The Muse will . . .

- offer specific fixes and craft observations: "This paragraph would work well as an intro."
- focus on writing as process, understanding the piece will grow.
- ask questions like "Is Michael the same character who was Charlie on page 25?"
- give emotional responses: "This moves me."

Your efforts to become good at critiquing will serve the writing of others—and your own.

CRITIC VIGILANCE

Guard against the voice of the Critic. Harsh or blanket statements do not belong in workshops and can poison a group.

BRAIN MATTER

Complete It: Label the comments as the Muse or the Critic:

_____ It's just the same as every other Tolkien wannabe.

_____ I liked your first piece better.

_____ I can't see where the characters are standing.

Explain It: In your own words, describe the difference between good critiques and the Critic.

WORKSHOP GUIDELINES

Giving strong and helpful critiques is a learned skill. As we grow in our knowledge of story craft and practice, we better articulate what we experience as readers of another's work.

The following suggestions are adapted from guidelines used in an MFA-level workshop instructed by Bruce Holland Rogers.[1]

The Writer's Workshop Tasks

Before Workshop

- Ready a solid draft; workshops aren't for first drafts or unrevised work.
- The story may have broken places where you need another's help.
- Use a manuscript format with page numbers.

During Workshop

- Sit apart from the group, if possible. This common practice may feel strange initially.
- Bring a duplicate copy to record comments.
- Remain silent. To curb defensiveness, many workshops do not allow the writer to speak until after the workshop.
- Listen intently. Are patterns of craft strengths and weaknesses emerging?
- Record questions for clarification.
- At the end, ask questions and/or take a vote to test shared opinion.

After Workshop

- If possible, first recover from the terror of being workshopped. Take a cool down.
- Expect contradictory comments. Hunt for patterns.
- Ponder your response: heed the comments, ignore them or take the suggestions in the opposite way. In other words, allow your creativity to interact with the workshop comments.

The Reader's Workshop Tasks

Before Workshop

- Be a reader, not an editor. Your goal is to experience the story and comment—not to embark on an error hunt.
- Record comments.
- Try to record at least four comments per page.

- Include both positive and negative comments.
- If possible, use craft terms (e.g., "good use of action beats").
- On the last page, record your name and email, in case questions arise.
- Effective endings: State predominant strength and weakness.

During Workshop

- Adhere to the Golden Rule: Discuss thy neighbor's writing how thou desires thine own writing to be discussed.
- To avoid a showdown, don't directly address the writer; instead say "the author."
- Remember that while you are serving the author, the writer is sovereign and may or may not take your suggestions.
- Avoid comparing the work to other group work. Even saying, "I loved this piece!" if you haven't said so for others can discourage.

After Workshop

- When the workshop ends, resist the temptation to continue to tell the author what you think he or she should do.
- Remember the writer may feel overwhelmed and may need time to decompress.

WORKSHOP FORMATS

There are many approaches and configurations of workshop formats. Some proven ones follow:

Read Aloud. This popular method has the writer read his or her work to the critique group who record comments and then discusses it. One downside: oral interpretation hides flaws.

Socratic. Leader asks questions that are answered by the workshoppers.

Clarion. Each group member explains their responses through the piece. When finished, the speaker says, "Pass." This works well in small groups.

The Modified Clarion. Selected members cover every response, positive and negative.

The Whidbey. Three members explain with examples what they see as the work's strongest strength and weakest weakness.

Classroom. The group discusses as a whole any point brought up. Fierce debates can arise, giving the writer a sense of the prevalence of opinion. Classroom works well in mature groups.

Free-for-all. Anyone can speak or debate, including the writer. This method works well at the end of a workshop that has used a more structured approach. Functions well in mature groups.

Good Cop-Bad Cop. The group member will offer one point of feedback—positive if a "good cop" or negative if a "bad cop." Go around the table, alternating each turn.

SECTION VII

The Wrap

RESOURCES FOR THE JOURNEY

If I were on a deserted island—washed ashore with an old typewriter and a zillion usable typewriter ribbons, boxes of dry paper, food and drinkable water—and could only have one book about writing, which would I choose?

The Art of War for Writers by James Scott Bell. This book is a gulp of Popeye's spinach. Its subtitle says it all: "fiction writing strategies, tactics and exercises." Nonfiction writers could benefit, too, from Bell's pep talks.

My favorite writing helps from this book:

1. Compile a Writing Improvement Binder.
2. Take a writing Sabbath—every week.
3. Write a set quota six days a week.

(About that #3? I didn't know I could. I could, and I did.)

If I could pick a second? Jane Friedman's *The Business of Being a Writer.*

MORE RESOURCES

Writer's Digest. Available online and in print. *Writer's Digest* has a wide and credible kingdom. You'll find books, conferences, on-line classes and a magazine available. Excellent for learning about the publishing business and genre writing.

Writer's Market. This thick tome is published annually and gives readers updated names of editors, publishers, contests and magazines. The first few pages also equip writers with an extensive chart on what to charge and information on how to write queries. Many public libraries carry a copy.

Poets & Writers Magazine. This magazine serves the literary writer. It is also concerned with funding writers and education. The back section offers want ads that range from editors for unpublished manuscripts to fellowships and grants, writing conferences and retreats, etc.

SUGGESTED READING

You may find these books worthy companions for your writing journey.

CREATIVE SOUL CARE

Cameron, Julia. *The Artist's Way: A Spiritual Path to Higher Creativity.* New York: Penguin Putnam Inc., 1992, 2002.

> Cameron's twelve-week workbook was groundbreaking in the creativity movement. It still helps many. To keep my creativity green, I cycle through it every couple of years.

Gilbert, Elizabeth. *Big Magic: Creative Living Beyond Fear.* New York: Riverhead Books, 2015.

Goldberg, Natalie. *Writing Down the Bones.* 30th Anniversary ed. Boulder: Shambhala, 2016.

Perini, Don. *Emerge: Study Guide.* Grand Rapids: Orange Press One, 2015.

Wright, Vinita Hampton. *The Soul Tells a Story: Engaging Creativity with Spirituality in the Writing Life.* Downers Grove, IL: Intervarsity Press, 2005.

PROCESS COMPANIONS

Bell, James Scott. *The Art of War for Writers: Fiction Writing Strategies, Tactics, and Exercises.* Cincinnati: Writer's Digest Books, 2009.

Clark, Roy Peter. *Help! for Writers: 210 Solutions to the Problems Every Writer Faces.* New York: Little, Brown and Company, 2011.

George, Elizabeth. *Write Away: One Novelist's Approach to Fiction & the Writing Life.* New York: HarperCollins Publishers, 2004.

James, Steven. *Story Trumps Structure.* New York: Writer's Digest Books, 2014.

Lamott, Anne. *Bird by Bird: Some Instructions on Writing and Life.* New York: Anchor Books, 1994.

See, Carolyn. *Making a Literary Life: Advice for Writers and Other Dreamers.* New York: Random House, 2002.

Sellers, Heather. *Chapter after Chapter.* Cincinnati: Writer's Digest Books, 2007.

White, Fred. *Where Do You Get Your Ideas?* Cincinnati: Writer's Digest Books, 2012.

> Professor White offers various worksheets that facilitate idea-generation for book projects.

REVISING BOOKS

Bell, James Scott. *Revision & Self-editing: Techniques for Transforming Your First Draft.* Cincinnati: Writer's Digest Books, 2008.

Browne, Renni and Dave King. *Self-editing for Fiction Writers: How to Edit Yourself into Print.* 2nd ed. New York: HarperCollins, 2004.

> Many agents want writers to comb through this book before submitting a manuscript.

Stein, Sol. *Stein on Writing.* New York: St. Martin's Press, 1995.

> For fiction and nonfiction writers.

CRAFT COMPANIONS

Ackerman, Angela and Becca Puglisi. *The Emotion Thesaurus: A Writer's Guide to Character Expression.* CyberWitch Press, 2012.

Bell, James Scott. *Plot & Structure: Techniques and Exercises for Crafting a Plot that Grips Readers from Start to Finish.* Cincinnati: Writer's Digest Books, 2004.

Burroway, Janet, Elizabeth Stuckey-French, and Ned Stuckey-French. *Writing Fiction: A Guide to Narrative Craft.* 8th ed. Boston: Longman, 2011.

> Burroway's craft textbook is considered the best. Excellent resource.

Byle, Ann. *Christian Publishing 101: The Comprehensive Guide.* Grand Rapids: Credo House Publishers, 2018.

Dunne, Peter. *Emotional Structure: Creating the Story Beneath the Plot.* Sanger, CA: Quill Driver Books, 2008.

Frey, James N. *How to Write a Damn Good Novel.* New York: St. Martin's Press, 1987.

Gerke, Jeff. *Plot Versus Character: A Balanced Approach to Writing Great Fiction.* Cincinnati: Writer's Digest Books, 2010.

Knight, Damon. *Creating Short Fiction.* New York: St. Martin's Griffin, 1997.

> This book contains a strong explanation of POV.

Leland, Christopher. *The Art of Compelling Fiction: How to Write a Page-Turner.* Cincinnati: Story Press, 1998.

Maass, Donald. *The Breakout Novelist.* Cincinnati: Writer's Digest Books, 2010.

———. *The Emotional Craft of Fiction.* Cincinnati: Writer's Digest Books, 2016.

———. *Writing 21st Century Fiction.* Cincinnati: Writer's Digest Books, 2012.

McKee, Robert. *Dialogue.* New York: Twelve, 2016.

———. *Story: Substance, Structure, Style and the Principles of Screenwriting.* New York: HarperEntertainment, 1997.

Vogler, Christopher. *The Writer's Journey.* Studio City: Michael Wiese Productions, 2007.

> This book famously updates the Hero's Journey by Joseph Campbell.

NONFICTION CRAFT

Karr, Mary. *The Art of Memoir.* New York: HarperCollins, 2015.

Lopate, Phillip. *To Show and To Tell: The Craft of Literary Nonfiction.* New York: Free Press, 2013.

Miller, Brenda and Suzanne Paola. *Tell It Slant: Creating, Refining and Publishing Creative Nonfiction.* New York: McGraw Hill, 2012.

Moore, Dinty W. *Crafting the Personal Essay.* Cincinnati: Writer's Books Digest, 2010.

Stanek, Lou Willett. *Writing Your Life: Putting Your Past on Paper.* New York: Avon Books, 1996.

Zinsser, William. *On Writing Well: The Classic Guide to Writing Nonfiction.* 6th ed. New York: HarperPerennial, 1998.

> Long considered a "bible" for nonfiction writers.

THE WRITING BUSINESS

Friedman, Jane. *Publishing 101: A First-time Author's Guide to Getting Published,*

Marketing and Promoting Your Book and Building a Successful Career. MBA for Writers, 2015.

———. *The Business of Being a Writer.* Chicago: University Press of Chicago, 2018.

Jane Friedman is the trusted voice in all things publishing. Listen to Jane.

Guide to Literary Agents. Cincinnati: Writer's Digest Books. (Annually updated.)

Hyatt, Michael. *Platform: Get Noticed in a Noisy World.* Nashville: Thomas Nelson, 2012.

This is the go-to book for building one's platform.

Levinson, Jay Conrad, Rick Frishman and Michael Larsen. *Guerrilla Marketing for Writers: 100 Weapons for Selling Your Work.* Cincinnati: Writer's Digest Books, 2001.

Morris, Tee and Pip Ballantine. *Social Media for Writers: Marketing Strategies for Building Your Audience and Selling Books.* Cincinnati: Writer's Digest Books, 2015.

Excellent book full of simple and thorough how-to's on using social media as a writer.

Rein, Jody and Michael Larsen. *How to Write a Book Proposal.* 5th ed. Cincinnati: Writer's Digest Books, 2017.

A savvy how-to on book proposals.

The Practical Writer. Ed. Therese Eiben and Mary Gannon. New York: Penguin Books, 2004.

This collection of essays offers important guidance in everything from submission strategies to editor etiquette and bookstore appearances.

ENDNOTES

CHAPTER 1

1. Walter Wangerin Jr., (lecture, Evangelical Free Church, Walker, MI, 1992).
2. *Doctor Zhivago,* directed by David Lean (Beverly Hills: Metro-Goldwyn-Mayer, 1965), DVD.
3. Catherine Marshall, *Christy* (New York: Avon Books, 1967), 101.
4. Anna Akhmatova, "Instead of a Preface," *Against Forgetting: Twentieth-Century Poetry of Witness,* ed. Carolyn Forche (New York: W.W. Norton & Company, 1993), 101-2.

CHAPTER 2

1. Vinita Hampton Wright, *The Soul Tells a Story* (Downers Grove: InterVarsity Press, 2005), 11.
2. Julia Cameron, *The Artist's Way: A Spiritual Path to Higher Creativity* (New York: Penguin Putnam, Inc., 2002), 21.
3. Frank Gruber, *Zane Grey: A Biography* (Roslyn, NY: Walter J. Black, Inc., 1969), 20.
4. Elizabeth Gilbert, *Big Magic: Creative Living Beyond Fear* (New York: Riverhead Books, 2015), 253.
5. Ibid.
6. Andrew Smart, *Autopilot: The Art & Science of Doing Nothing* (New York: OR Books, 2013).
7. James W. Pennebaker, *Opening Up: The Healing Power of Expressing Emotions* (New York: The Guilford Press, 1990), 35.
8. Cameron, *The Artist's Way,* 9.
9. Ibid., 159-160.
10. Julia Cameron, *The Right to Write: An Invitation and Initiation into the Writing Life* (New York: Putnam, 1998), 80.
11. Elizabeth Scott, "Perfectionistic Traits: Do They Sound Familiar?" *Very Well Mind,* March 1, 2018, https://www.verywellmind.com/

signs-you-may-be-a-perfectionist-3145233/.

12. Wanda Mutschler, "Bull's Eye," n.d.

13. Sleepless in Seattle, directed by Nora Ephron (Culver City: TriStar Pictures, 1993), DVD.

14. Romans 7:15-20.

15. Cameron, *The Artist's Way,* 154.

16. Dave Beach, "Cherish is the Word: Formation in the Creative Life" (Breathe Deeper Writing Retreat, Stanwood, MI, March 9, 2019).

17. Gregory Ciotti, "Loving the Process Means Everything for Creativity," *Psychology Today,* April 13, 2015, https://www.psychologytoday. com/blog/habits-not-hacks/201504/loving-the-process-means-everything-creativity.

CHAPTER 3

1. Teresa Torres, "What You Can Learn About Managing Creative Teams," INC.com, February 22, 2016, https://www.inc.com/teresa-torres/ what-pixar-can-teach-you-about-managing-for-creative-success.html/.

2. Elizabeth Ivy Hawkins, "Process," *100 Day Challenge* (blog) July 22, 2018, www.elizabethivy.com or @elizabethivyhawkins.

3. Anne Lamott, *Bird by Bird: Some Instructions on the Writing Life* (New York: Anchor Books, Inc., 1994), 19.

4. Ibid., 18.

5. James Scott Bell, *The Art of War for Writers* (Cincinnati: Writer's Digest Books, 2009), 18.

6. Elizabeth George (lecture, Whidbey, WA: Northwest Institute of the Literary Arts, 2013).

7. Fred White, *Where Do You Get Your Ideas?* (Cincinnati: Writer's Digest Books, 2012), 180-1.

8. Steven James, *Story Trumps Structure: How to Write Unforgettable Fiction by Breaking the Rules* (Cincinnati: Writer's Digest Books, 2014), 87, 94-5.

9. Elizabeth George. *Write Away: One Novelist's Approach to Fiction and the Writing Life* (New York: Harper, 2004).

10. Lamott, *Bird by Bird,* 21.

CHAPTER 4

1. James Scott Bell, "The Geyser Approach to Revision," *Writer's Digest*

Magazine 91, no. 5 (July/August 2011), 22.

2. Ibid.

3. Eudora Welty, "Death of the Traveling Salesman" in *Shadow & Light: Literature and the Life of Faith,* ed. Darryl Tippens, et al., 2nd ed. (Abilene, Texas: ACU Press, 2005), 215.

4. Daniel Tocchini (Breakthrough, Grand Rapids, 2004).

5. Tee Morris & Pip Ballantine, *Social Media for Writers* (Cincinnati: Writer's Digest Books, 2015), 121.

CHAPTER 5

1. Vinita Hampton Wright (lecture, Calvin College, Grand Rapids, 2003).

2. Anthony Doerr, *All the Light We Cannot See* (New York: Scribner, 2014), 12.

3. Lorilee Craker, *Anne of Green Gables, My Daughter & Me* (Carol Stream, IL: Tyndale Momentum, 2015), 168.

4. Ian McEwan, *Atonement* (New York: Doubleday), 74.

CHAPTER 6

1. *Levity,* directed by Ed Solomon (Culver City: Sony Pictures Classics, 2003), DVD.

2. Ann Hood, "Escapes," in *Three Genres,* ed. Stephen Minot, 9th ed. (Boston: Longman, 2012), 60.

3. Lori J. Carrell and Rudolph F. Verderber, *Communicate! Instructor's Resource Manual,* 8th ed. (New York: Wadsworth Publishing Company, 1996), 36.

4. Sarah Stone and Ron Nyren, *Deepening Fiction: A Practical Guide for Intermediate and Advanced Writers* (New York: Pearson Longman, 2005), 137.

5. Tom Clancy, *The Sum of All Fears* (New York: G.P. Putnam's Sons, 1991), 141.

6. Stone and Nyren, *Deepening Fiction,* 139.

7. Maeve Binchy, *Tara Road* (New York: Delacorte Press & Random House, 1998), 314.

8. Donald Maass, *Writing 21st Century Fiction* (Cincinnati: Writer's Digest Books, 2012), 2.

9. Steven James, conversation with author, October 2015.

CHAPTER 7

1. William Goldman, n.d., n.p.
2. Martha Kay Salinas, "Moving Beyond Stereotypes," (blog) June 9, 2018, www.marthakaysalinas.com.
3. Ann Hood, "Escapes," 54, 58.
4. "The Legend of Rambaldi," *Alias* special feature, http://alias.wikia.com/wiki/The_Legend_Of_Rambaldi.
5. Angela Ackerman & Becca Puglisi, *The Emotion Thesaurus: A Writer's Guide to Character Expression* (CyberWitch Press, 2012).
6. Saul A. McLeod, "Unconscious Mind," *Simply Psychology,* 2015, April 23, 2019, http//www.simplypsychology.org/unconscious-mind.htm.
7. Donald Maass, *The Breakout Novelist: How to Craft Novels that Stand Out and Sell* (Cincinnati: Writer's Digest Books, 2010), 88.

CHAPTER 8

1. *North and South,* directed by Brian Percival (United Kingdom: BBC One, 2004) DVD.
2. Bruce Holland Rogers, Craft of Fiction Class (Northwest Institute of the Literary Arts, Whidbey Island, WA, 2011).
3. R. J. Palacio, *Wonder* (New York: Alfred A. Knopf, 2012).
4. Steven Johnson, "Watching TV Makes You Smarter" in *They Say, I Say,* ed. Gerald Graff, et al., 2nd ed. (New York: W.W. Norton & Company, 2012), 282.
5. Renni Browne and Dave King, *Self-Editing for Fiction Writers: How to Edit Yourself into Print,* 2nd ed. (New York: HarperCollins, 2004), 43-4.
6. Andy Scheer, *Christian Publishing 101: The Comprehensive Guide to Writing Well and Publishing Successfully,* ed. Ann Byle (Grand Rapids: Credo House Publishers, 2018), 38.
7. Linnae Conkel, email to author, November 30, 2018.
8. Ibid.

CHAPTER 9

1. Jacquelyn Mitchard (lecture, Northwest Institute of the Literary Arts, Whidbey Island, WA, August, 2013).
2. Rogers, Craft of Fiction Class.

3. Stone and Nyren, *Deepening Fiction,* 73.

4. Jeff Gerke, *Plot Versus Character: A Balanced Approach to Writing Great Fiction* (Cincinnati: Writer's Digest Books, 2010), 190-1.

5. Ibid., 196.

6. Ibid., 195.

7. Joseph Bates, *The Nighttime Novelist* (Cincinnati: Writer's Digest Books, 2010), 114.

8. Ibid.

9. K. M. Weiland, *Structuring Your Novel* (Scottsbluff, NE: Pen for a Sword, 2013), 78.

10. Ibid., 91.

11. Ibid., 94.

12. Ibid., 115.

13. Rogers, Craft of Fiction Class.

14. *The Mentalist,* directed by Bruno Heller (Sacramento: Primrose Hill Productions, 2008-2015), DVD.

15. Christopher Vogler, *The Writer's Journey,* 3rd ed. (Studio City: Michael Wise Productions, 2007), 9.

16. *The Last Ship,* directed by Hank Steinberg, et al. (Santa Barbara: Channel Road Productions, 2014-2018) DVD.

17. John Updike, "Pigeon Feathers" in *Shadow & Light: Literature and the Life of Faith,* ed. Darryl Tippens, et al., 2nd ed. (Abilene, Texas: ACU Press, 2005), 329-352.

18. Ben Nyberg, *One Great Way to Write Short Stories* (North Light Books, 1988).

CHAPTER 10

1. *Numb3rs,* Nicholas Falacci and Cheryl Heuton (Los Angeles: Scott Free Productions, 2005-2010) DVD.

2. Sol Stein, *Stein on Writing* (New York: St. Martin's Griffin, 1995), 92.

3. Caleb Dierolf, "Class Exercise on Competing Script," Advanced Fiction Workshop (Cornerstone University, Grand Rapids, fall 2017).

4. Nevil Shute, *A Town Like Alice* (New York: Ballantine Books, 1950).

5. *Merriam-Webster* On-line, s.v. "fair cow."

CHAPTER 11

1. "The Anatomy of a Scene: Train Fight," *Alias* special feature, season 4.

2. Stein, *Stein on Writing,* 254.
3. Abby Wakeman, "Class Exercise," Introduction to Creative Writing (Cornerstone University, Grand Rapids, fall 2017).
4. *Snow White and the Seven Dwarfs,* Walt Disney, et al. (United States: Buena Vista Film Distribution, 1937), DVD.
5. Sharon Oard Warner, "A Simple Matter of Hunger," in *Three Genres,* ed. Stephen Minot, 9th ed. (Boston: Longman, 2012), 95.

CHAPTER 12

1. Janet Burroway, Elizabeth Stuckey-French and Ned Stuckey-French, *Writing Fiction: A Guide to Narrative Craft,* 8th ed. (Boston: Longman, 2011), 210.
2. Ibid.
3. Julie Cantrell (lecture, Breathe Christian Writer's Conference, Grand Rapids, fall 2014).

CHAPTER 13

1. *Galaxy Quest,* directed by Dean Parisot (Universal City: DreamWorks Pictures, 1999), DVD.
2. Glenn Arnold, "Readability Chart," Feature Writing Class (Wheaton College Graduate School, Wheaton, 1989).
3. Steven James, *Placebo* (Grand Rapids: Revell-Baker Publishing Group, 2012), 154.
4. Elizabeth Okma, *Hired for War,* Class Assignment, Fiction Writing (Cornerstone University, Grand Rapids, fall 2018).
5. Marilynne Robinson, *Gilead* (New York: Farrar, Straus and Giroux, 2004), 3.
6. Taylor Branch, *Parting the Waters: America in the King Years, 1954-1963* (New York: Simon & Schuester, Inc., 1988), 882.
7. Gary D. Schmidt, *Lizzie Bright and the Buckminster Boy* (New York: Houghton Mifflin Harcourt, 2004), 63.
8. Elizabeth Gaskell, *North and South* (Ware, Britain: Wordsworth Classics), 262.
9. Brian Doyle, "Joyas Voladoras," in *The Norton Reader,* ed. Linda Peterson, et al., 13th shorter ed. (New York: W.W. Norton & Company, 2012), 291.
10. Savanna DeWolf, "The Magic Encounter," Class Assignment,

Introduction to Creative Writing (Cornerstone University, Grand Rapids, 2015).

11. Heather Sellers, *The Practice of Creative Writing: A Guide for Students* (New York: Bedford/St. Martin's, 2008), 101.

12. Scott Russell Sanders, "Under the Influence" in *The Norton Reader,* ed. Linda Peterson, et al., 13th shorter ed. (New York: W.W. Norton & Company, 2012), 60.

13. Ellen Douglas, *Can't Quit You Baby* (New York: Penguin Publishers, 1988).

14. Eudora Welty, "Death of the Traveling Salesman" in *Shadow & Light: Literature and the Life of Faith,* ed. Darryl Tippens, et al., 2nd ed. (Abilene, Texas: ACU Press, 2005), 256.

15. Cynthia Beach, *The Surface of Water* (Grand Rapids: Soul Seasons Publishing, 2019), 319.

16. Frank E. Peretti, *Prophet* (Wheaton, Ill.: Crossway Publishers, 1992), 122.

CHAPTER 14

1. Lorilee Craker, email to the author, October 3, 2012.
2. Vitaly Friedman, "White Space and Simplicity: An Overview," *Smashing Magazine,* January 12, 2007, https://www.designernews.co/stories/50332-white-space-and-simplicity-an-overview/.
3. Ibid.
4. Ibid.
5. Mark Boulton, "Whitespace." *A List Apart,* January 9, 2007, https://alistapart.com/article/whitespace/.
6. Katherine Applegate, *The One and Only Ivan* (New York: HarperCollins Children's Books, 2012).
7. Karen Hesse, *Out of the Dust* (New York: Scholastic Press, 1997), 60.
8. Nicholas Wolterstorff, "The Grace that Shaped My Life" in *Hearing the Call* (Grand Rapids: William B. Eerdmans Publishing Company, 2011), 14.

CHAPTER 15

1. Beach, *The Surface of Water,* 191.
2. Rogers, Craft of Fiction Class.
3. *Cinderella Man,* directed by Ron Howard (Universal City: Universal

Pictures, 2005), DVD.

4. Stone and Nyren, *Deepening Fiction,* 107.

5. Ibid., 107.

6. Marjorie Sandor, "On Leaving Florida" in *Three Genres,* ed. Stephen Minot, 9th ed. (Boston: Longman, 2012), 18.

7. Arrival, directed by Denis Villeneuve (Hollywood: Paramount Pictures, 2016), DVD.

8. Beach, "Prologue" in *The Surface of Water,* 4.

CHAPTER 16

1. Tracy Groot, email to author, February 5, 2011.

2. Ibid.

3. Sarah Domet, "Outlining: Choosing the Best Outline Method for You" *The Writer's Digest* 91, no. 1 (January, 2011): 60-62.

4. Stein, *Stein on Writing,* 278.

5. Ibid., 279-281.

6. Ibid., 281.

7. Ibid., 281-282.

8. Ibid., 282-283.

9. Ibid., 284-285.

10. *Sully,* directed by Clint Eastwood (Burbank: Warner Bros. Pictures, 2016). DVD.

CHAPTER 17

1. Pew Research Center, "Belief in God," accessed December 17, 2018, http://pewforum.org/religious-landscape-study/belief-in-god/.

2. David R. Beach, "Jesus, Man of Sorrows: Using Suffering Well in Fiction and Nonfiction" (lecture, Breathe Christian Writer's Conference, Grand Rapids, fall 2015).

3. "Writing Tips," on Francine Rivers' official website, accessed August 6, 2018, http://francinerivers.com/writing-tips/.

4. Ibid.

5. Gary D. Schmidt, conversation with author, June 22, 2018.

6. Davis Bunn, "The Christian as Artist," in *The Making of a Christian Bestseller,* ed. Ann Byle (Grand Haven: FaithWalk Publishers, 2006), 14.

7. Hannah VanKampen, email to author, January 6, 2018.

8. Schmidt.

CHAPTER 18

1. Harrison Ford, interview, *Parade* (July 7, 2002).

2. Flannery O'Connor, "Revelation" in *Shadow & Light: Literature and the Life of Faith,* ed. Darryl Tippens, et al., 2nd ed. (Abilene, Texas: ACU Press, 2005), 306-7.

3. Richard Rohr, *Everything Belongs: The Gift of Contemplative Prayer* (New York: The Crossroad Publishing Company, 2003), 118.

4. Beach, *The Surface of Water,* 22.

5. Rogers, Craft of Fiction Class.

6. Louise Erdrich, *The Last Report on the Miracles at Little No Horse* (New York: Perennial, 2001), 42-43.

CHAPTER 19

1. Jim Connelly, email to author, 2013.

2. Ibid.

3. Roy Peter Clark, *Writing Tools: 50 Essential Strategies for Every Writer* (New York: Little, Brown and Company, 2006), 196.

4. Ibid.

5. Iris Graville, "Writing in a Bulletproof Vest," irisgraville.com (blog), a later version of the post published in The Wayfarer Magazine (March 20, 2018). Author of *Hiking Naked: A Quaker Woman's Search for Balance* (Homebound Publications, 2017).

6. Frank Gruber, *Zane Grey: A Biography* (The World Publishing Company, 1969), 176.

7. Loren Grey, foreword to *The Vanishing American,* by Zane Grey (New York: Pocket Books, 1982), vi.

8. Ian Herbert, "Revealed: Why Brocklehurst's Inspiration Threatened to sue Brontë." *The Independent,* May 25, 2006, https://www.independent. co.uk/news/uk/this-britain/revealed-why-brocklehursts-inspiration-threatened-to-sue-bronteuml-479611.html/.

9. Ibid.

10. Steve Hendrix, "Publishers Hated 'A Wrinkle in Time': Madeleine L'Engle Never Forgot Rejections" in *The Washington Post,* March 10, 2018, https://www.washingtonpost.com/news/retropolis/wp/2018/03/10/

publishers-hated-a-wrinkle-in-time-madeleine-lengle-never-forgot-the-rejections/

11. Ibid.

CHAPTER 20

1. Joseph Heller, Google, n.d.
2. John Moir, *The Writer's Market* (Cincinnati: Writer's Digest Books, 2006).
3. Prov. 27:6, *The NIV Study Bible,* New International Version, ed. Kenneth Barker (Grand Rapids: Zondervan Bible Publishers, 1985), 983.
4. Cameron, *The Artist's Way,* 38.
5. Ibid., 38-39.

CHAPTER 21

1. Robert Frost, "The Road Not Taken," accessed December 17, 2018, https://www.poets.org/poetsorg/poem/road-not-taken.
2. Jane Friedman, *The Business of Being a Writer* (Chicago: The University of Chicago Press, 2018), 137.
3. Olivia Markham, "Delilah Marvelle: Making the Choice to Switch" in *Guide to Self-Publishing,* ed. Robert Lee Brewer, revised ed. (Cincinnati: Writer's Digest Books, 2014), 177.
4. Kathleen Kerr, email to author, July 21, 2015.
5. Patti Hill, telephone conversation with author, March 2018.
6. Zetta Elliot (keynote address, Writer's Digest IndieLAB, Cincinnatti, September 29, 2018).
7. Kathleen Horning, "I See White People" (CCBC blog) http://ccblogc.blogspot.com/2013/07/i-see-white-people.html. February 1, 2019.
8. Elliot.

CHAPTER 23

1. Bruce Holland Rogers, "Some Notes on Workshop Criticism," Fiction Workshop Class (Northwest Institute of the Literary Arts, Whidbey Island, WA, 2010). Adapted with permission.

INDEX

PERMISSIONS

"In the terrible years...." from "Requiem 1935-1940" by Anna Akhmatova; English translation from *Poems of Akhmatova,* Selected, Translated and Introduced by Stanley Kunitz with Max Hayward (Mariner Books, an imprint of Houghton Mifflin Harcourt 1997). Copyright © 1967, 1968, 1972, 1973 by Stanley Kunitz and Max Hayward. All rights reserved. Used with permission.

Excerpt taken from *The Artist's Way: A Spiritual Way to Higher Creativity* by Julia Cameron, copyright © 1992, 2002 by Julia Cameron, pp. 158-160. Used by permission of Tarcher, an imprint of Penguin Publishing Group, a division of Penguin Random House LLC. All rights reserved. Used with permission.

Excerpt taken from Elizabeth Ivy Hawkins, 2018, www.elizabethivy.com and @ elizabethivyhawkins. Used by permission of Elizabeth Ivy Hawkins.

Excerpt taken from *Anne of Green Gables, My Daughter & Me* by Lorilee Craker, © 2015, p. 168. Published by Tyndale Momentum, an imprint of Tyndale House Publishers, Inc., Carol Stream, IL 60188, www.tyndalemomentum.com. Used by permission of Lorilee Craker.

Excerpt taken from Martha Kay Salinas © 2018, www.marthakaysalinas.com. Used by permission of Martha Kay Salinas.

Excerpt taken from *Christian Publishing 101* by Ann Byle, © 2018, p. 38. Published by Credo House Publishers, a division of Credo Communications LLC, Grand Rapids, MI, credohousepublishers.com. Used by permission of Ann Byle.

Excerpt taken from *Placebo* by Steven James, © 2012, p. 154. Used by permission of Revell, a publishing division of Baker Publishing Group, P.O. Box 6287, Grand Rapids, Michigan, www.revellbooks.com.

Excerpt taken from *Lizzie Bright and the Buckminster Boy* by Gary D. Schmidt, © 2004, p. 63. Published by Sandpiper, an imprint of Houghton Mifflin Harcourt

ABOUT THE AUTHOR

Cynthia Beach is a longtime creative writing professor, writer and coach who studied creativity under Dr. Eric Maisel and is a certified spiritual director. Her articles, short stories and contributions appear in newspapers, literary journals and books like *Hope in the Mourning Bible* (Zondervan), *Horse of My Heart* (Revell) and *Media Ethics* (Longman). She is a reviewer for *The Englewood Review of Books* and has over a hundred articles published in Seattle and Grand Rapids newspapers. She has a journalism masters from Wheaton College and a masters of fine arts from the Northwest Institute of the Literary Arts. She cofounded the Breathe Christian Writers Conference and founded the writing retreat, Breathe Deeper. *The Surface of Water,* a novel, will be available fall, 2019. She lives near Grand Rapids, Michigan on a quiet seven acres with her husband, Dave. For more information, please visit www.cynthiabeach.com.

AVAILABLE FALL, 2019

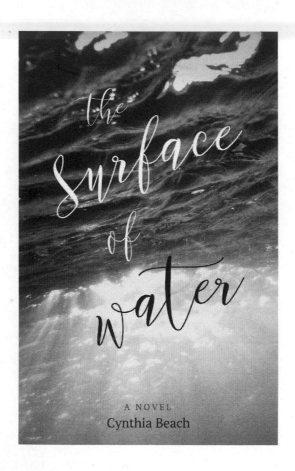